Getting to Grips with English Grammar

Year 3

Brilliant
PUBLICATIONS

Charlotte Makhlouf

We hope you and your pupils enjoy using the ideas in this book. Brilliant Publications publishes many other books to help teachers. To find out more details on any of the titles listed below, please go to our website: **www.brilliantpublications.co.uk**.

Getting to Grips with English Grammar, Years 1–6

ISBN:	Year 1:	978-1-78317-215-3
	Year 2:	978-1-78317-216-0
	Year 3:	978-1-78317-217-7
	Year 4:	978-1-78317-218-4
	Year 5:	978-1-78317-219-1
	Year 6:	978-1-78317-220-7

Also by the same author is **Brilliant Activities for Reading Comprehension, Years 1–6**

ISBN:	Year 1:	978-1-78317-070-8
	Year 2:	978-1-78317-071-5
	Year 3:	978-1-78317-072-2
	Year 4:	978-1-78317-073-9
	Year 5:	978-1-78317-074-6
	Year 6:	978-1-78317-075-3

Published by Brilliant Publications Limited
Unit 10
Sparrow Hall Farm
Edlesborough
Dunstable
Bedfordshire
LU6 2ES, UK

www.brilliantpublications.co.uk

The name Brilliant Publications and the logo are registered trademarks.

Written by Charlotte Makhlouf
Cover design by Brilliant Publications Limited
Cover photograph: hanging upside down;
Victor Gladkov (Shutterstock, Inc)

© Text Charlotte Makhlouf
© Design Brilliant Publications Limited
Illustrations Paula Martyr (GCI Illustration Ltd)

Printed ISBN: 978-1-78317-217-7
ePDF ISBN: 978-1-78317-224-5

First printed and published in the UK in 2019.
Updated March 2019.
10 9 8 7 6 5 4 3 2 1

Contents

Theme 5 – Forest Holiday Park

Theme 6 – Giant's Weekly

Getting to Grips with English Grammar, Year 3
© Charlotte Makhlouf and Brilliant Publications Limited

Introduction

Grammar is important because it is part of our everyday communication. It helps us to be understood and to make our communication more effective, clear and powerful. It is a tool through which we can express ourselves. Teaching grammar effectively can give children the confidence to develop their skills much faster. It is believed to develop:

- attention and concentration
- language comprehension
- expressive skills
- reading and writing
- storytelling
- thinking skills

For those children for whom English is a second language, or for those who might be learning a new language, proper grammar is essential as all languages follow grammatical patterns. Grammar develops a skill for life, which flows into all areas of their lives. Future jobs may very well be dependent on the ability to communicate thoughts or ideas effectively, or present information logically and coherently.

Sadly, however, many of our grammar experiences are viewed as tedious. Many exercises are just pages of drills and the concept of grammar as being fun or exciting is eradicated. These books are designed to give children more confidence with their grammar. They have a range of exciting themes, filled with imaginative ideas, which will transport children through a grammatical journey that is fun and action-packed.

The comprehension activities at the beginning of each theme serve two purposes: they help to set the context for the activities that follow and they introduce key grammatical concepts. These activities demonstrate how grammar is used in context and provide excellent talking points for introducing and reinforcing the grammatical point being studied.

Within each theme there are opportunities for expanding children's writing. These activities are useful for assessing whether children can transfer the grammar points they have learned into their own writing. Mini quizzes at the end of each theme are designed to 'test' how much they have remembered.

Within each class there will be a variety of abilities. Less able pupils may need to have the instructions read and discussed with them prior to doing the activity. The Challenges at the bottom of each page allow more able children to be stretched and provide activities for faster finishers.

The books are linked to the requirements of the National Curriculum of England, where a knowledge of the correct terminology is also implicit.

Help your pupils get a firm grip on grammar and punctuation with this photocopiable six-book series, *Getting to Grips with English Grammar* for Years 1–6!

Cross-curricular Activities

For children to gain a firm grasp of grammar and punctuation, it is important that the skills are not just taught in isolation; they need to be practised and reinforced across the curriculum. The chart below provides suggestions for how key grammar skills introduced in this book can be reinforced through different curriculum areas. Some of the history and geography activities relate to topics in the National Curriculum for England.

Grammar skill	Cross-curricular Activity
Word Families	**Art** Be creative: design and make a new plant species for Giant Gryn's garden (see pages 13–23): Make plant pots from polystyrene squares covered in brown paper. Write root words on the pot. Make stems from pipe cleaners and cut out weird-shaped leaves and attach them to the pipe cleaner. Write words you can make from the root word on the leaves. **English** Choose a word family of your own and write a description of a new, dangerous tree that Giant Gryn has found on a remote mountainside. Use as many words from the family as you can to describe the new tree.
Using Prefixes	**English** Make up some new names for some dangerous plants in Giant Gryn's Garden (see page 17). Using different prefixes, write what the plant is like. For example: stable – unstable: the Greenback Plant is very <u>unstable</u> in cold weather.
Noun Phrases	**Geography** Look at a map of the world and decide on places from which Giant Gryn might have found some new and exotic plants. Mark them on the map and then draw a picture for each plant with its name underneath. Give a description of each plant.
Nouns	**Art and English** Draw or make large treasure chests and then list all the nouns which can be found inside (see Captain Codfish pages 24–31). Perhaps you could put your list on parchment-style paper or make it look like an old parchment. **Maths** Having found an old treasure chest, imagine that you are Captain Codfish doing an inventory of the price of each thing inside it (see page 25). Make up a price list. Use the price list to work out the value of each digit (place value). Make up some problems for a friend using the price list. For example: What would the cost of three rings be at £75 each?

Collective Nouns	**English** Ask the children to make up collective nouns of their own for different animals (see page 29). Make all the ideas into a booklet with pictures. The children could also make up their own collective nouns for the weather. For example: A dazzle of lightning. Illustrate these or make them into little hanging mobiles.
Using a, an or the	**Art and English** Make an advent calendar and inside each window draw a little picture and write inside – a ring, a star, an apple, the Kings, for example.
Abstract Nouns	**Mindfulness** Draw a sea picture of your own with plenty of detail in it and write as many different abstract nouns as you can in the pictures (see page 28). Photocopy it and give it to a friend to colour. **History** Imagine that you are Howard Carter and you have found the tomb of Tutankhamun. Use abstract nouns to describe your feelings when you opened the tomb. Draw large-sized pictures of some of the Egyptian gods and make them look like a particular abstract noun eg anger, lust, love, despair …
Reported Speech	**History** Write a letter to a famous historical person using reported speech to tell them what you have been doing recently.
Past Tense	**History** Imagine that you are Julius Caesar. Write a diary extract giving an account of the invasion of Britain using past tense. Alternatively, the children can imagine that they are writing a diary extract from the point of view of one of the Anglo Saxons. **Geography** Design a map for Captain Codfish showing one of the areas around which he had some adventures (see pages 24–31). Put little descriptions of what happened at each point using past tense. For example: Dogneck Bay – this is where we were attacked by pirates and the Jolly Seasnail was wrecked.
Imperative Verbs	**English and Computing** Imagine that you are Doctor Gloom and you are trying to organise a new programme to tell Bobot how to make a cup of tea, or make a cake (you decide) (see page 37). Use imperative verbs for your instructions. When you are happy with your instructions and you have checked them, why not write them out neatly or type them up. **Design and Technology** Design the new 'Cookbot' for Doctor Gloom (see page 32) and write powerful imperative verbs around it to say what it can do. You could make it both 2D and 3D.

Imperative Verbs (cont.)	**Drama** Recreate the Bottville Fair (see page 36). Imagine that you are the different inventors. Think of something to say about your invention and try to sell it to the crowd. Do a demonstration for the crowd. Ask one of your friends to be the robot and give it commands using imperative verbs.
Using Speech Marks	**History** Get together with a friend and research a famous person together. Using speech bubbles write some questions and answers for that famous person.
Speech Marks	**English** Imagine that you are a reporter who is interviewing Doctor Gloom (see page 33). Write down some questions for him about Bobot and then respond to the questions imagining that you are the Doctor – use speech marks. With a friend, make up a conversation between two superheroes. Each person can take on the role of a different/or a made up superhero. Use speech marks to track the conversation. Then transform the conversation into a comic book format, putting the speech into speech bubbles and drawing pictures to go with the dialogue. **Speaking and Listening and Drama** Interview one of the trolls (see page 76). One child can be the interviewer and one the troll. Ask them questions about the recent troll troubles. Record the conversation or video it and then write up what the troll said using reported speech and speech marks, ready to go into the Giant's Weekly Newspaper. **Drama and PSHE** Ask the children to imagine that they are giants at a meeting in their Town Hall, trying to discuss what to do about the Troll Troubles. Perhaps some of the children can be trolls. Have a discussion about what they can do to solve the problem. Perhaps one child can be the Chairperson
Present Perfect Tense	**English** Draw a big Bobot of your own on paper and then add some speech bubbles around it with some statements using the present perfect tense (see pages 41–42). **Drama** Imagine that you are a translator for an alien who has just come to the planet. Translate what the alien is saying using the present perfect tense. For example: He says he has been to London.

Prepositions	**Design and Technology** Make a little police station out of a shoe box (see PC Brown's Police Station pages 45–55). Use paper and cardboard to put various things inside like tables and chairs and pictures, etc. Make a little list to go with the box using prepositions of place to say where things can be found. For example: The picture is above the telephone. **Geography** Make a town map of the area in which PC Brown is in charge. Say where the shops, houses, church, Police Station and other places can be found. Add roads. Be imaginative. Use prepositions of place to describe where certain places are, for example: The church is behind the cinema.
Synonyms	**English** Give each child a strip of paper. Ask them to write a sentence on it. For example: The weather outside is horrible. The paper is then passed to the next person who has to identify the adjective in the sentence and then find another word (synonym) for it. The weather outside is horrible: horrible – dreadful! (See pages 51–52.) Use an extract from a well-known book and highlight specific words. Ask the children to think of a synonym for those highlighted words. Make a bingo board of words and then the children have to identify synonyms for the words on their boards. For example, one board may have the following words on it: pretty, kind, useful, small, big. The teacher might read out a card with the word 'huge'. Children have to identify this with one of the words on their board which means the same.
Antonyms	**Art and English** Make some jewellery necklaces with some antonyms on them (see page 53). You can start the chain with one jewel and then the next jewel in the chain should be an antonym for it. See how long you can make the chain. For example: lovely, hideous, gorgeous, repulsive, etc. You can vary the antonyms and start a new trail with a different coloured gem to show it's a new start in the chain. **Geography** Look at a variety of different famous mountains. Think of a word to describe one of the mountains and then suggest an antonym for each describing word. For example: Mount Everest – small/huge, freezing/hot. You could put your antonyms in little clouds and colour those that are true descriptions of the mountain, in blue. For example: small/huge – you would colour 'huge' in blue. **English** Write a newspaper review on the Green Forest Holiday Park (see pages 56–66). Imagine that you are staying there and have interviewed various guests. Give a review of it. Make up an exciting headline, picture, caption for the picture, etc.

Conjunctions	**English** Imagine that the Green Forest Holiday Park has opened up some brand new activities (see pages 56–66). For example: quad biking and trekking by horse around the park. Give a description of each activity using as many time and cause conjunctions as you can within your description. You could either write it up neatly or use a computer to type it up. **Circle Time** Make some posters for some classroom rules using conjunctions of time and cause. **Speaking and Listening** Have a class conversation which involves using conjunctions to put sentences together. Go around the class and add to the sentence. For example: Person 1: I love going to the shops. Person 2: but I prefer going to the cinema. Person 3: I like wearing jeans, Person 4: however, I don't like wearing dresses. Have a pile of cards with conjunctions on them. Give a child a card and they have to make up a sentence containing that conjunction. For example: 'because'. I love going to the fair because there are so many great rides. Make it into a class competition.
Contractions	**English and Art** Make a small flap book showing the contractions and what their full version is. For example: we've – we have. You could decorate the book. You could perhaps make the book for a younger class to show them what they mean and put speech bubbles inside with animals saying something using the shortened form. For example: a giraffe might have a speech bubble coming from his mouth and inside it says: "I'm very tall!" – I am very tall. **Drama** Prepare a speech for the opening of the Green Forest Holiday Park (see pages 56–66), in which you use contractions. For example: 'I'm standing here outside the amazing Green Forest Holiday Park where we've …' The speech could be for a news reporter or for the manager of the Holiday Park. Once prepared, you can deliver it to your class.
Adverbs	**Drama** Imagine that you are Tina behind the reception desk (see page 60). In groups, you could take on the role of different customers at the Green Forest Holiday Park and the person being Tina has to respond to them in a particular way. You could have fun with this by putting a variety of adverbs on cards and giving them to people so that they have to say things in a particular way. For example: On the card is the word 'stupidly' or 'miserably', one of the children has to say something to Tina in the style of the word they have been given. For example: 'The swimming pool is very cold today.' (to be said 'stupidly').

Adverbs (cont.)	**Drama and English** Imagine you are the director of the Dillcombe Players (see page 61). Write an excerpt of the play they are performing. Set it out correctly in play format and use plenty of adverbs to show how the lines should be delivered by the actors. As director, you could work with a group of friends to perform the excerpt.
Adverbs of Time	**English** Imagine you are one of the smugglers (see page 62). Give an account of one of your secret landings at Dillcombe Bay. Use adverbs of time to say when events happened. **Geography** Look at a map of England and research the special coastal areas where smuggling took place and plot them on the map. Write notes beside them to explain what happened there.
Adverbs of Cause	**English and Art** Draw some posters promoting safety at the beach (see page 64). Use adverbs of cause to describe what may happen if you don't follow the rules of the beach. **Other languages** Change the posters into French, Spanish, etc, so that there are translations for visitors to the beach.
Reported Speech	**English** Devise a new story for the newspaper 'Giant's Weekly' (see pages 67–82)). Use reported speech to describe what has happened and then give the news article an appropriate headline, picture and caption for the picture.
Paragraphs	**English** Imagine that you are a new giant/giantess who has designed a fantastic new range of clothing (see page 69). Use paragraphs to describe your range, what it is like, who it might appeal to, etc. Write some letters to Giant Groan, the Editor in Chief of 'Giant's Weekly', giving your views on the troll situation or explaining about something that has happened recently. Don't forget to use paragraphs.
Subordinate Clauses	**History** Look at some historical events involving the Romans, Anglo Saxons or Vikings. Take an event and then add a subordinate clause to give more information about it. For example: The Romans brought us underfloor heating, which helped to make homes warmer and more civilised. Put all the events and clauses together into a little booklet about the Romans/Anglo Saxons/Vikings.

Subordinate Clauses (cont.)	**English** Take a simple statement, such as – I like eating cake. Then expand it through different subordinate clauses to make it more interesting. Have a class competition to see who can make the most entertaining sentence altogether. For example: I like eating cake, especially cakes filled with jam and cream.
Homophones	**English** Brainstorm as many different homophones as you can and then make a little booklet with pictures to show what they mean. For example: deer and dear – you could draw a picture of a fallow deer and then the other picture could be of a letter with the opening words 'Dear ... ' **Geography** Imagine that you are Captain Codfish and you have found a new map of a strange land (see pages 24–31). Look at a map of the world and try and work out where this new land might be situated. Then make up some instructions for where the treasure can be found or make up a short history about the new land using a variety of homophones which are incorrect for the meaning you want. Ask a friend to decode the instructions so that they make sense. For example: *Deer friends, I am hear at the beech wear I have found ...*
Headings and Subheadings	**Mindfulness** The giants are very stressed out by the recent troubles (see page 78). Ask the children to think of ways in which they can relax. Perhaps they can turn their ideas into a book/booklet with an illustrated front and back cover and title. They may like to extend the activity by adding headings and subheadings with extra information.
Metaphors	**English** Ask the children to think of the elements and devise their own metaphors to describe the wind/water/rain/thunder/lightning, etc (see page 80). Ask the children to create a new superhero of their own. Think of their superpower and then describe it with a metaphor. For example: He was a lion, charging through the bush.
Past and Present Tense	**History and English** Compare the past with the present. For example: I went to Legoland last year. (past) I have a cat called Fluffy. (present) The Romans had spears and shields. (past) My Mum and Dad have a car. (present)

Giant Gryn's Garden

A **word family** is a group of words which are related to each other: such as sweet, sweeter, sweetly. All have the root word 'sweet'.

Giant Gryn has given some information about his garden. Highlight all the word families you can find in the information below. Choose a different colour for each family.

Gobbler fungi

Gobbler Fungi make excellent medicine. They have great medicinal value. In the giant's medical world, the Gobbler Fungi is used to treat a variety of illnesses. Giant Paramedics keep a bagful of this medication with them at all times!

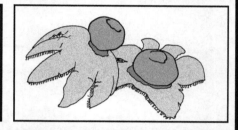

Mrs Grizzlekin

Mrs Grizzlekin gives me help in the garden. She loves plants so she is very helpful. I listen to her talking to the plants asking them to forgive her for forgetting to give them water! The Talkiwalki Plants will reply, "you are forgiven!"

Bat Cave

My bat cave needs a lot of care. The bats are a bit of a headache as they need special attention. I have a night time head torch, which I wear in the cave along with some other headgear to protect my head. I check the bats to see where they are heading each evening to catch their food. When I know where they are headed I write it down in my Bat Log Book.

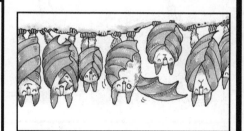

Challenge

Can you make word families using these root words?

play   **real**   **happy**   **sign**

Can you add a prefix and a suffix to the same word? For example, sign – de**sign**ed

Frugal Berry Theft

The Snap Rats are stealing all the frugal berries from Giant Gryn's frugal berry pond. The trouble is they are only looking for the berries from the same word family. Can you cut out the ones you think the Snap Rats will want and stick them on the pond? (Take care not all the words are real words – some are made up!)

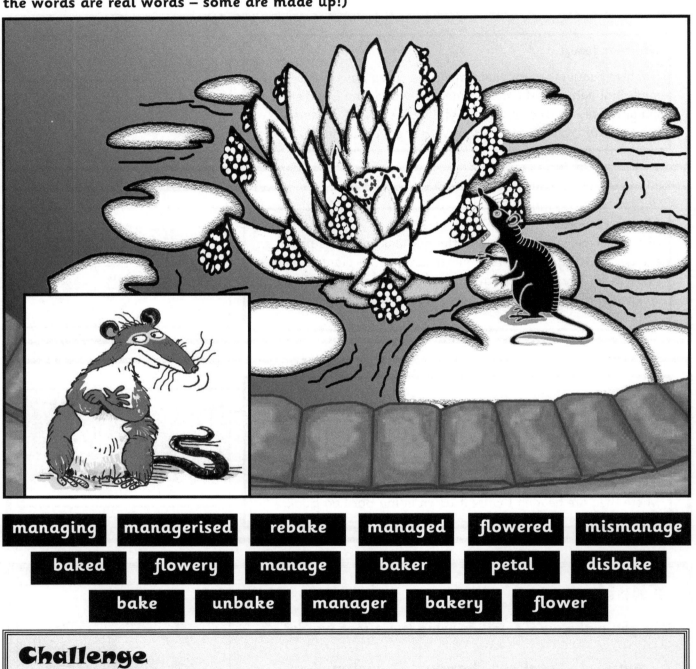

| managing | managerised | rebake | managed | flowered | mismanage |

| baked | flowery | manage | baker | petal | disbake |

| bake | unbake | manager | bakery | flower |

Challenge

Make a frugal berry pond of your own. Choose three of the word families from below. How many words can you make from the three root words? Stick them in your frugal berry pond.

| love | port | take | joy | cook | wrap |

Getting to Grips with English Grammar, Year 3

Plant Sort

Giant Gryn is sorting his plants. Can you help him to find the word families? Colour each family a different colour to help you.

Write the word families out in the chart below. The first has been done for you.

help					

Challenge

Identify the two word families in the following letter. Then circle the words which aren't real. Can you substitute them with real words?

Dear Giantess Gwinn,

Thank you so much for the beautiful photographs of the Twizzle Plant. I didn't realise you were such a great photographer! The Twizzle plant is really photogenic, I love the way it is smiling for the photo! I was writing to let you know I have invented a new plant growing machine. I think it is a great invention which will be a wonderful invantage for all gardeners! I have been inventing things for years and thought that, as you love plants, you might like to know about my inventing and the disvents I have been making.

Yours faithfully
Giant Gryn

In the Potting Shed

Homophones – these are words which sound the same but mean something different. They can also be spelt differently.

Giant Gryn has a list of jobs to be done. Some of the words he has used are incorrect. Can you spot them using the words from the list? The first one has been done for you.

Don't forget to ~~by~~ new Snorkweed seeds.

buy

_____

Do not let the dog berry its bone!

_____

Meat Giantess Gwenda at the post office.

_____

meet	buy
bury	rain
flower	plain
suite	bear
hole	

Water the small pink flour by the pond.

_____

Repair the whole in the shed roof.

_____

Clean the 3-piece sweet in the lounge

_____

Look for Niki's teddy bare in the garden.

_____

Buy plane buns for the picnic.

_____

There has been no reign to water the plants.

_____

Challenge

Giant Gryn is VERY excited. He has found an ancient parchment hidden under the old, oak tree. He is struggling to read it because some of the words sound the same but are not the correct meaning. Can you help him correct the words?

Written this day in the rein of Good Queen Bessie, may peace be upon her sole. Four eye Giant Thickbeard the Grate leave to the finder of this parchment some treasure! Eye have sailed around the whirled and scene such sites though the whether has often bean pore. Giant waves, the site of witch wood make a groan mail shake. You will find the treasure under the old oak ...

Getting to Grips with English Grammar, Year 3

Jabberjoot Leaves

Giant Gryn has been collecting jabberjoot leaves. Use these prefixes to change the root words on Giant Gryn's jabberjoot leaves. Put the new word on the leaf beside it. The first has been done for you.

un– mis– dis–

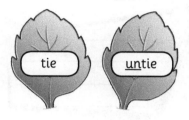

tie — untie

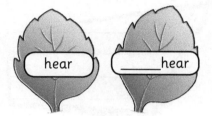

hear — _____hear

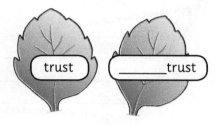

trust — _____trust

clear — _____clear

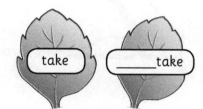

take — _____take

miss — _____miss

il– im– in–

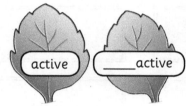

active — _____active

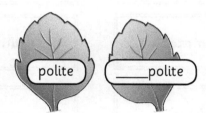

polite — _____polite

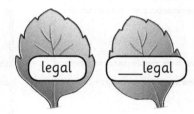

legal — _____legal

Challenge

Draw a large beanstalk with some jabberjoot leaves of your own. Write the words below on the leaves. Use the prefixes in the black box to change the words. Put the new words on the leaves you have drawn.

faithful   justice   patient

helpful   possible   adequate

may   comfortable   balance

in– im–
un– dis–

At the Garden Centre

A **prefix** is a small word that goes at the start of a word. It can change the meaning of the **root word**.

Because Giant Gryn's garden is so special, he has to visit the garden centre a lot! This week he needs to buy some different parts for his garden equipment. Can you help him sort out what he needs to buy and put them into the correct shopping trolley?

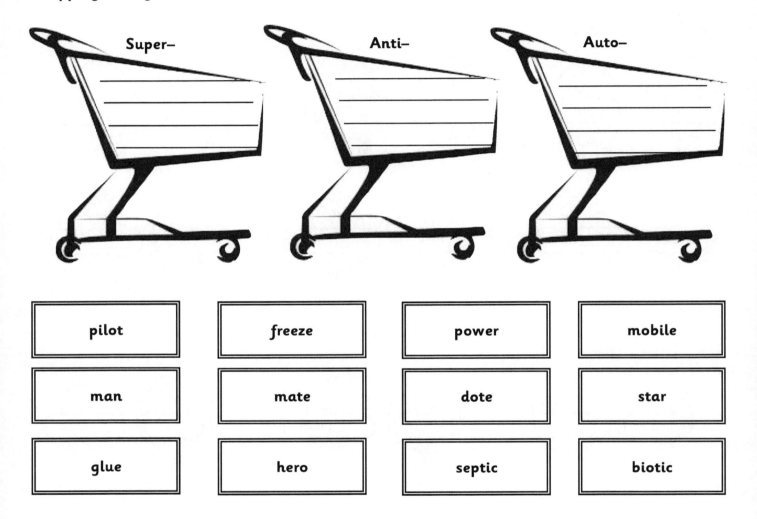

Super–   Anti–   Auto–

pilot	freeze	power	mobile
man	mate	dote	star
glue	hero	septic	biotic

Challenge

Giant Gryn is very confused by the words. He does not know what they mean. Can you make a little booklet to help explain to him what each word means and how they can be used in a sentence? It might be helpful to him if you could illustrate it too!

Autoroute

Meaning: An autoroute is a fast motorway for vehicles.
Sentence: The autoroute was very busy this morning.

Getting to Grips with English Grammar, Year 3

In the Garden

> We use 'a' before a word beginning with a **consonant** for example: a cat. We use 'an' before a word beginning with a **vowel**. For example: an elephant.

Giant Gryn has many exciting things in his garden. He has made a list. Can you put 'a' or 'an' before the words?

____	dragonfly
____	pond
____	butterfly
____	ant
____	Creekle tree
____	apple tree
____	deck chair
____	egg
____	iguana
____	leaf
____	Oogle bird
____	olive bush
____	winkle fish
____	tractor
____	compost heap

Giant Gryn has a lot of dangerous plants and animals in his garden. Mrs Grumble is trying to get the garden closed down. She has written a letter to the council. Can you fill in the correct articles: 'a', 'an' or 'the'?

Dear Councillor Chuff,

I think Giant Gryn's garden should be shut down! It is __ dangerous place. It has ____ poisonous Dooklesnap plant and __ area filled with snakes that bite. On ___ tops of ____ Twit Bushes are deadly spikes. I have __ cat called Fluffy who likes to go in ____ garden. I am scared he will have ____ accident there! There should be __ sign telling people how dangerous it is. Even the butterflies are ____ danger! Their wings have ____ itchy dust on them which can drop on your skin.

I look forward to hearing from you on this matter.

Mrs Grumble

In the Garden

We use 'a' before a word beginning with a **consonant** for example: a cat. We use 'an' before a word beginning with a **vowel**. For example: an elephant.

Challenge

Imagine that you are Councillor Chuff. You have to respond to Mrs Grumble's letter. Using as many of the words and phrases listed below as you can, write a letter of your own, explaining what an amazing garden it is and how it should be looked after to protect all these exciting plants and creatures.

- an exciting place
- a very special winkle fish
- a memory tree
- the only garden with an Oogle bird
- an amazing garden
- a Dooklesnap Plant
- a safe haven
- a protected place
- a six leafed clover
- a rare breed of ...

Dear Mrs Grumble,

_____

_____

_____

_____

_____

_____

_____

_____

_____

_____

_____

_____

_____

Getting to Grips with English Grammar, Year 3
© Charlotte Makhlouf and Brilliant Publications Limited

New Plants

Fill in the missing articles.

| a   an |

_____ Dooklesnap Plant

_____ Itwit Plant

_____ Ogg Bush

_____ Snot Snap Plant

Fill in the missing articles.

| a   an   the |

Gump Weed

Gump Weed grows in _____ pond. It has ___ awful smell! It can be used in __ nice salad or in ___ sandwich. Gump Weed takes ___ short time to grow. In _____ winter it turns purple. It is not ___ dangerous weed. When ___ weather is hot it can be used as ___ umbrella!

Dooklesnap Plant

_____ Dooklesnap plant is ____ deadly one. Do not touch _____ leaves or they will make you itch badly. They like to be kept in ___ very hot place but not directly in _____ sun. Plant in _____ ground when it is 4 inches high.

Dear Giantess Grunt,

   Thank you for _____ beautiful Giffgo Tree. It is ___ amazing tree. I love all _____ little butterfly-shaped berries it has. I have put it in ___ cool spot in ___ garden.

   I am sending you __ cutting from my Scooter Bush Plant. It has __ lovely smell in summer. If you squash _____ leaves into ___ paste, it makes ___ excellent after sun cream. It likes to be in ___ sunny spot in _____ garden. Give it __ lot of water.

   Hope to see you soon.

Love Giant Gryn xx

Challenge

Imagine that you are Giantess Grunt. Write back to Giant Gryn explaining how well the Scooter Bush Plant is doing. Underline all the articles you use (a, an or the).

Giant Gryn's Open Garden

Giant Gryn is planning on opening his garden to the public. He is making a beautiful leaflet to tell people all about the plants and creatures in his garden. Can you help him write it? Try to be as imaginative as you can! Don't forget to draw some pictures!

Flystick Bush

_____

_____

_____

_____

_____

_____

_____

_____

Welcome

Welcome to my beautiful garden. I hope you will enjoy wandering around it.
Please do not touch the _____
_____ in the garden and do wear the protective gloves, hat and mask provided when around the _____

The Creekle Trees

These trees are ancient. When they creak it means they are talking. If you put your hands carefully on the bark you can hear them. Be careful what you whisper back to them. They are very friendly but they can get upset if you are rude.

The Oogle Bird

_____

_____

_____

_____

_____

_____

_____

Challenge

Draw a map of the garden and label all the areas and plants in it so that the visitors know where to find them.

Mini Quiz

Some of the creatures from Giant Gryn's garden have escaped and are running around the village. Use the correct article 'a' or 'an' to help PC Potter write down what is missing.

____ sneekle rat
____ peepo lizard
____ eagle butterfly
____ dwarf elephant
____ bat-eared rabbit
____ lion-headed squirrel

Correct PC Potter's report putting in either 'a', 'an' or 'the'.

I was on my way to ___ police station, when to my surprise I saw ___ huge rabbit jump out of __ dustbin and run down ___ road. It was closely followed by ___ green lizard. It was ___ awful shock. The villagers were in ___ terrible flap. It seems there was ___ hole in ___ garden fence. The animals made __ run for it. I called ___ animal officer who managed to catch ___ rabbit and ___ lizard and put them into ___ cage.

Giant Gryn has made a shopping list for himself. Can you identify his spelling mistakes and correct them?

■ a plane scone _____
■ plasters for my heal _____
■ new bawl for the dog _____
■ peace of cake _____
■ collect male from post office _____
■ bag of flower _____
■ some leaks for a soup _____
■ a pound of meet _____

Giant Gryn's cousin has been shopping! He has made some mistakes with his prefixes. Which prefix, 'super', 'anti' or 'auto' should be in front of the underlined words? Write out the passage correctly.

(super)   (anti)   (auto)

I drove my <u>anticar</u> on the <u>superroute</u> to get to the <u>antimarket</u>. I bought some <u>superfreeze</u> and a great <u>antibiography</u> on 'The Life of Giantess Gom'. She is a real <u>autowoman</u>! Some people say she has <u>antipowers</u>! I bought more <u>autoglue</u> and some <u>superbiotic</u> cream for my insect bites. Then I drove home.

_____
_____
_____
_____
_____
_____
_____
_____
_____

Captain Codfish

Highlight the common nouns – red.
Highlight the abstract nouns – yellow.
Highlight the proper nouns – green.
Highlight the collective nouns – blue.

> There are different types of noun:
> **common nouns** are ones you can see or touch: cat, dog, door.
> **abstract nouns** are nouns that you cannot see or touch but which represent feelings: love, hate, fear.
> **collective nouns** describe a group of things: a herd of cows, a bunch of flowers.
> **proper nouns**: are the names of people, countries or places; they all have capital letters.

The name's Codfish, Captain Codfish! I love sailing the high seas in my beautiful ship called the Jolly Octopus. She is my pride and joy! Sometimes we see dolphins and whales. I have a fine crew of sailors. We sail around the seas searching for treasure. I love golden coins, jewellery and fine necklaces. I have a monkey called Jim and a parrot called Mr Screecher. Our latest adventure was a hard one. The seas were rough and we lost the small jolly boat in a gale. The mast broke so we had to stop at a desert island covered in palm trees, to fix it. It was in the jungle that we came face to face with a fierce tribe of natives, who chased us through a forest of trees. We hid from them behind a waterfall where, to our great happiness, we found a chest of treasure filled with gold coins, silver rings, precious jewels and diamond bracelets. We carried it back to the Jolly Octopus, fixed the mast and set sail quickly for Beachcomber Bay.

Can you find all the nouns and write them in the correct boxes. One has been done for you.

Common Nouns
seas
_____
_____
_____

Abstract Nouns
_____
_____
_____

Collective Nouns
_____
_____
_____

Proper Nouns
_____
_____
_____

Challenge

Write a short story of your own to explain how Captain Codfish got his parrot, Mr Screecher.

Captain Codfish's Treasure Chest

Common nouns are everywhere – you can see and touch them!

Captain Codfish is making a list of all the things he has in his treasure chest, before he hides it on a desert island. Can you help him write a list?

_____
_____
_____
_____
_____
_____

| thoughts | daggers | | maps | hope | brooches |

lamps

coins

bury

goblets

| chains | blue | | find | pearls |

Challenge

Captain Codfish has bumped his head on the yardarm and lost his memory! He is trying to remember the name of some things but can't think what they are. Can you think of the words for him from his clues?

1. We drop this in the sea to stop the ship from moving. _____

2. This helps to move the ship along – it is big and white. _____

3. I store all my rum in this. _____

4. I can find this type of nut at the top of palm trees. _____

5. You can see this fluttering at the top of the mast. _____

6. This is a special piece of paper which tells me where to go. _____

Captain Codfish's Secret Map

> The names of people, places, street names, months and days of the week are **proper nouns**. They should all start with a capital letter.

Captain Codfish is trying to update his treasure island map. He has forgotten to put on the capital letters. Can you correct his list of directions and the labels below? Look at the map below and decide where Captain Codfish has hidden his treasure. Write out directions for Captain Codfish to follow so he can find his treasure again.

Map directions: bottlenose bay is at point 1, cuttlefish cove is at point 3, lobster lagoon can be found at point 4, shark reef is at point 2, palm tree oasis is at point 5, shipwreck bay is at point 6, cutlass cavern is at point 7 and sticky swamp is at point 8.

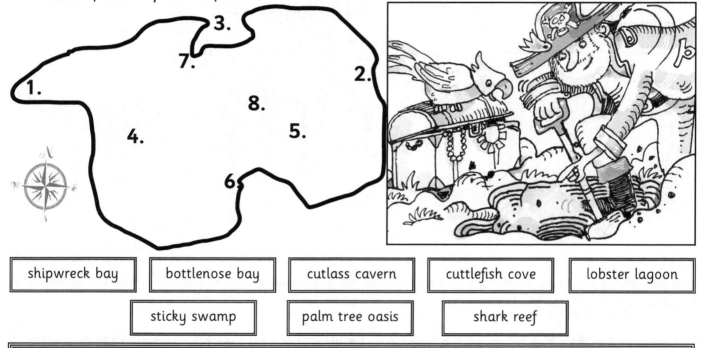

| shipwreck bay | bottlenose bay | cutlass cavern | cuttlefish cove | lobster lagoon |

| sticky swamp | palm tree oasis | shark reef |

Challenge

Captain Codfish has written a letter to his old sea pal Captain Redbeard. They had a lot of adventures together. Can you help Captain Codfish with his capital letters?

dear redbeard,

It is an age since I last saw you, when we sailed on the happy starfish together. do you remember the battle we had in cuttlefish cove when we sank captain cuttle's ship, the slippery octopus? those were the days, eh! old jim baines was in the dolphin inn the other day. we spoke of our adventures round skull bay. he told me that big sally has a new ship called the flying albatross. she lives near pirate cove.

i hope you are keeping well. look forward to seeing you soon.

captain codfish

Getting to Grips with English Grammar, Year 3

In the Harbour

Abstract nouns are nouns you feel but you can't touch or see them. Like 'love' or 'hate'.

Circle the boats with abstract nouns on them.

Captain Codfish likes to tell stories about his old ships. In this story, underline all the abstract nouns.

"The Jolly Octopus was a fine ship. Joy filled my heart when I sailed in her. She was my pride and love. She caused envy amongst the other pirates I can tell you! Their eyes would flash with hate when I sailed into the harbour. I felt sad when she hit rocks in Jumbaloo during a violent storm. Despair filled me! Anger too when I thought I'd never get another ship so grand. Then, we captured the Golden Jellyfish!"

Challenge

Imagine you are the fearsome Captain Snapper. You have just watched the Jolly Octopus sail into the harbour. Use all the abstract nouns in the box to write a short piece of writing describing how you felt when you saw this amazing ship! Be imaginative and creative!

jealousy
anger
fury
despair
love
happiness
excitement
wonder
hope
hate

_____

_____

_____

_____

_____

_____

Captain Codfish's Cavern

Light your way through the tunnel. Cut out and stick the abstract nouns on the lanterns and the common nouns on the rocks.

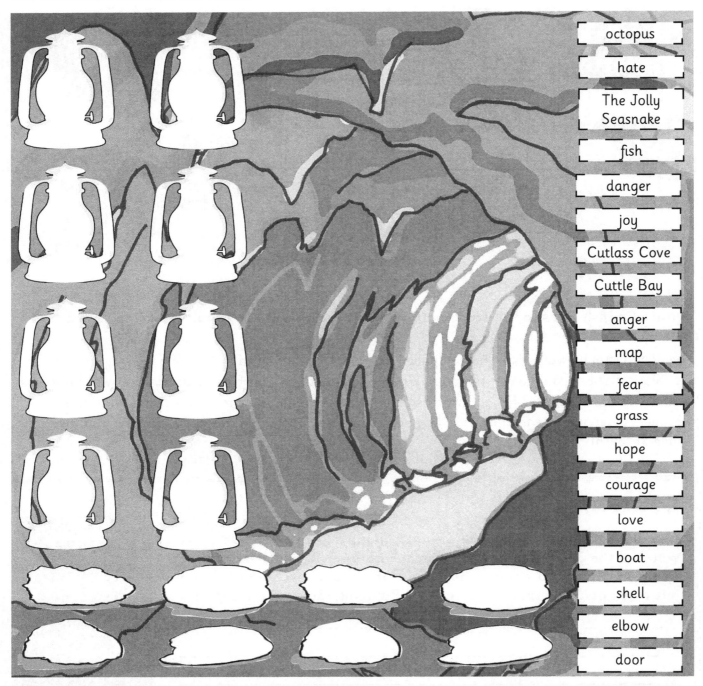

octopus
hate
The Jolly Seasnake
fish
danger
joy
Cutlass Cove
Cuttle Bay
anger
map
fear
grass
hope
courage
love
boat
shell
elbow
door

Challenge

Write four abstract nouns of your own.

1._____ 2._____ 3._____ 4._____

Getting to Grips with English Grammar, Year 3
© Charlotte Makhlouf and Brilliant Publications Limited

Ye Olde Sea Dog's Tavern

A **collective noun** is the name given to describe a group of things as one unit, for example, 'a group of sheep' are known as a 'flock'.

After having been at sea for a while, Captain Codfish enjoys relaxing at Ye Olde Sea Dog's Tavern with a glass of rum. Using the list provided, can you write the correct collective noun in the right box.

_____ of ships	_____ of lions	_____ of kittens
_____ of cards	_____ of flowers	_____ of birds
_____ of drawers	_____ of books	_____ of stairs

flock	fleet
flight	library
pride	litter
bunch	deck
chest	

Captain Codfish enjoys talking about all the things he has seen on his travels. Can you put in the correct collective nouns as he seems to have forgotten what they are.

"It was off Cape Coddle that I saw the _____ of enemy ships! I had been looking at a _____ of dolphins when I saw them. We headed for the Island of Rumba where a _____ of monkeys threw coconuts at us. We made camp under a whole _____ of stars. It was a wonderful sight. In the early morning a _____ of bees attacked us. Luckily we got back to the ship before they stung us. A _____ of birds flew overhead as we set sail for Nunking to exchange our cargo of spices for jewels and coins."

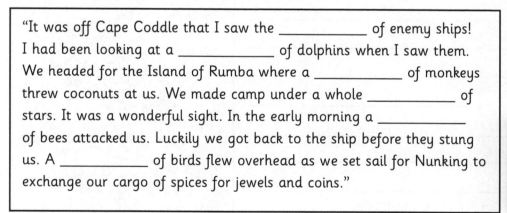

flock	swarm
troop	fleet
school	galaxy

Challenge

Write an exciting diary entry for Captain Codfish, for when he anchored off the African coast and had some adventures there. Use as many of the collective nouns in the box as you can.

a pride of lions	a bundle of firewood
a herd of elephants	a flock of birds
a shoal of fish	a bunch of bananas
a string of beads	a set of tools

Captain Codfish's Log

Captain Codfish likes to keep a diary (log) of all the things that happen at sea and on land. He's hoping that one day it might be made into a famous book! Here is his entry about the capture of the ship, *'The Dancing Walrus'*.

I, Captain Custard Codfish, will tell you of the battle between myself and my arch enemy, Slippery Sal. Slippery Sal is the meanest pirate around. Her ship, 'The Dancing Walrus' was the envy of other pirates with its forty guns. I had my eye on that ship too. Jealousy burned in me for it was a beauty. One dark night, Slippery Sal attacked my ship, 'The Golden Jellyfish'. Panic gripped us as they fired burning cannon balls at us. Despair filled us as the fire took hold. But Slippery Sal had made a foolish mistake. When she wasn't looking, we swung ourselves over to 'The Dancing Walrus', cut the grappling hooks and set sail with Sal left stuck on the burning 'The Golden Jellyfish'. We felt sadness watching the Jellyfish burn, but Sal will come after us I know, for revenge!

Imagine that you are Slippery Sal and that you have managed to survive the burning of 'The Golden Jellyfish'. Write a diary entry of your own, describing how you got away and what revenge you are planning!

Mini Quiz

Highlight all the common nouns – blue. Highlight the proper nouns – green.
Highlight the collective nouns – red. Highlight the abstract nouns – orange.

Mr Screecher is a clever parrot. He used to live with a flock of parrots on a small island. Mr Screecher is friends with Jim the monkey. Jim is very naughty. He steals apples and bananas from the ship's kitchen when Mr Stiggle, the cook, isn't looking. Mr Stiggle is preparing an evening feast on the shore of Beachcomber Bay. There will be a big camp fire. Mr Stiggle is cooking lobsters and fish on the fire. A huge bundle of firewood is near the fire. All the pirates are filled with joy at the thought of a party. Out at sea, Pirate Pete is watching a big pod of whales. The whales have found a shoal of tiny fish to eat.

Fill in the blanks with the correct collective noun.

1. A _____ of grapes. 2. A _____ of puppies. 3. A _____ of books.

4. A _____ of cows. 5. A _____ of cards.

Cut and stick the different nouns from the bottom of the page into the correct headings.

Abstract Nouns	Common Nouns	Collective Nouns	Proper Nouns

ship	anger	peace	Coconut Cove
a pod of whales	Mr Screecher	shell	Pirate Pete
a bunch of keys	sand	a troop of monkeys	hope
joy	island		Captain Cork

Bobot the Robot

A fantastic new robot has been built by Doctor Gloom. "I have called the robot, 'Bobot'," he told reporters. "Bobot is going to change the way household chores are done. He will make life easier for everyone because he will do all the work."

Bobot was revealed at the annual Robot Fair in Bottville. "I love the way he responds to commands so quickly," Professor Benny Simms told reporters. "Bobot is a really clever robot; he seems almost human."

Doctor Gloom took three years to make Bobot. "He can cook, clean, sew and do all your household chores," Doctor Gloom told excited crowds at the Bottville Robot Fair.

"I am planning to create another robot that will only be used for cooking. It will be able to create any meal you want!" For those people who hate cooking, this is good news. "I'm going to buy the new robot as soon as it comes out," housewife Melia Graves told reporters. "I hate cooking!" Doctor Gloom plans to call the new robot 'Cookbot'.

Bobot's most exciting feature is his ability to sort and scan the washing. "It means you will never have to worry about mixing your white and dark items," explained Doctor Gloom.

The Doctor was pleased with the response from crowds at the Fair. "It is very positive." His newest robot will be launched in 2024.

If you could ask Doctor Gloom some questions about the robot, what would you ask him? Write your questions in the speech bubbles. Then write what you think Doctor Gloom might say in return.

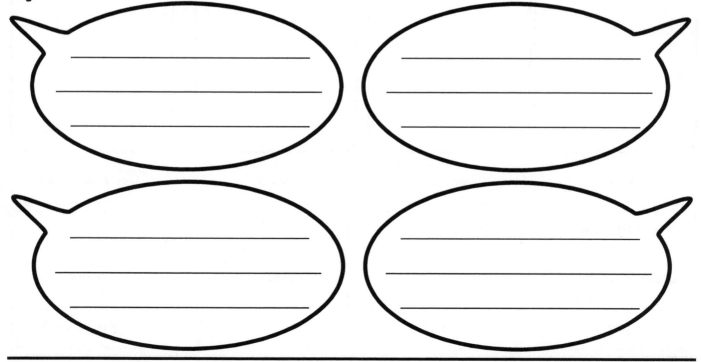

Getting to Grips with English Grammar, Year 3

Bobot the Spy

Bobot the Robot has been at a party secretly recording conversations.
Can you rewrite the conversations adding all the missing speech marks?

1. What a marvellous party this is, said Delly Davis. I've had a lot of fun.

_____
_____
_____

2. I've literally danced all night, squealed Lilly Lemon. My feet are going to drop off!

_____
_____
_____

3. I think I've talked too much, grinned Gavin Grokkle. I can hardly speak.

_____
_____
_____

4. I thought the dancers looked amazing, gasped Gilly Jines. Their outfits were gorgeous!

_____
_____
_____

5. I won the competition for the best outfit, smiled Lenny Luckless.

_____
_____

6. I don't normally win competitions, he added.

_____

7. Did I leave my coat at the party? asked Gwen Diddle.

_____

Bobot in Japan

Bobot has been flown all the way to Japan to show some important investors what he can do. One of the investors has written down everything Bobot has said, however, in his excitement, he has forgotten to put in the speech marks. Can you correct his notes?

I can cook and sew, explained Bobot. When you are tired, I can cook supper, said Bobot. I am programmed to be very helpful, added Bobot with a bow.

I am able to run a bath, said Bobot, without letting the bath water overflow!

Bobot told us, I am the most useful Robot in the world because I can do everything.

Doctor Gloom is a brilliant scientist, said Bobot. He has programmed me so that I can do the gardening, he added. When I am ready, I will be able to drive a car, Bobot smiled.

The investors are discussing Bobot. They think he is incredible! What do you think they are saying? Don't forget to add speech marks. The first has been done for you.

"What an astounding invention," exclaimed Yuri Takimoto. "It will change the world!"

_____
_____
said Yemi Surisan _____
_____

_____
_____
shouted Yuko Yamada
_____

_____
cried Toki Mikiyaki
_____

_____
_____
replied Mano Sujisawa
_____

_____
_____
agreed Chi Chong _____
_____

Challenge

Make up a secret conversation between two new investors. They are plotting to steal Bobot the Robot. Don't forget to use speech marks correctly.

Getting to Grips with English Grammar, Year 3

Bobot the Robot Factory Tour

> **Indirect** or **reported speech** tells people about a conversation that has already happened. For example: **direct speech** "That was difficult!" said Louise. **Indirect speech**: Louise said that it was difficult.

Doctor Gloom has taken Bobot to an important factory. The television news has reported what Bobot said at the factory. Turn what Bobot says into indirect speech. The first has been done for you.

"I am the best robot in the World," said Bobot.	Bobot said that he was the best robot in the world.
"I have many exciting functions," explained Bobot. "I have supersonic suction pads on my hands."	
"When I am tired," said Bobot, "I whirr very gently for five minutes. This gives you time to recharge me."	
"I will never get rusty," Bobot said happily. "This means I last even longer."	
"Doctor Gloom is programming me to drive," added Bobot. "This will be difficult."	
"I am easy to store," explained Bobot. "I think my dishwashing function is the best."	

Challenge

Imagine that you are a television presenter and you are delivering a brief report on Bobot's recent factory visit. Use all the indirect speech from above to help you write your report.

Bottville Robot Fair

A lot of people at the Bottville Robot Fair have commented on Bobot and how wonderful he is. Doctor Gloom has written down some of their comments. In his excitement, all the speech marks have been forgotten. Can you put them in? The first has been done for you.

> "I love the fact that he does ALL the washing,"
> said Mrs Boon excitedly.

> I think the best feature is his hoover hands,
> said Gary Grinling excitedly.

> How long did it take you to make Bobot?
> asked Jane eagerly.

> I like the way all the dials are covered up,
> explained Robin Smooth.

> Will it be difficult to clean Bobot? asked an old lady.

> Daisy stared at Bobot, he's really amazing. I love
> his shiny green metal; it's so pretty.

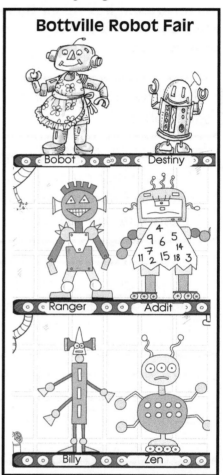

Bottville Robot Fair

Bobot · Destiny · Ranger · Addit · Billy · Zen

Challenge

Other inventors have commented on Bobot during a big inventors' meeting. Terry Brown, the Chairman, has written down all their comments. He has, unfortunately, forgotten all the speech marks in his eagerness to get the comments down. Can you put them in?

This is an incredible invention, said Professor Dull in amazement. The world of housework has changed forever, he continued excitedly. Professor Edwards told the meeting, I am so proud of Doctor Gloom. He is an amazing man. Doctor Swan said, this robot does everything, even the washing up! She continued, it doesn't even get rusty in water. Professor Bird told the meeting, Bobot is the perfect size for a robot. Professor Dull was worried, will Bobot like being put away in a cupboard at night? He seems very human. Doctor Gloom told fellow inventors, Bobot can also be used as a lamp so you can have him in a corner of your sitting room!

Giving Bobot Commands

> Some verbs give direct instructions, they are known as **imperative verbs** (bossy verbs).

Bobot the Robot needs commands to make a cup of tea. Can you write out the following commands in the correct order so that he can make the tea? The first has been done for you.

Pour the tea into a teacup.

Pour the boiling water from the kettle into the teapot.

Put the kettle on to boil.

Get the teapot out of the cupboard.

Put some teabags in the teapot.

Allow the tea to brew in the teapot.

Fill the kettle with cold water from the tap.

Add milk and sugar to taste.

1. _____Fill the kettle with cold water from the tap._____

2. _____

3. _____

4. _____

5. _____

6. _____

7. _____

8. _____

Challenge

Doctor Gloom needs Bobot to be able to do some gardening. Can you give Bobot some commands, to help him plant a sunflower seed. Use the imperative (bossy) verbs in the box, to help you.

_____

_____

_____

_____

_____

_____

take
fill
put
plant
place
give
press
smooth
water

Help Bobot Sort

Commands begin with an **imperative verb** (bossy verbs).

Bobot needs to be able to sort commands and statements. Sometimes he gets confused. Can you help him sort the following commands and statements into the right areas of Bobot's computer? The first has been done for you.

Commands	Statements
	We are going on holiday.

We are going on holiday.   Wash the dishes carefully.   I am going to have a bath.

This fish tastes lovely.   I have a new bike.   Take the tea out of the packet.

Give the dog a bath.   Scrub the potatoes.   The water is very hot.

Write two statements of your own.

Write two commands of your own.

Challenge

Mr Brown has just ordered a new Bobot the Robot of his own. Design a leaflet that will help Mr Brown to look after his new robot properly. The leaflet should have FOUR commands telling him what to do to look after the robot. It should also have FOUR statements telling him four things the robot can do to help him.

Getting to Grips with English Grammar, Year 3
© Charlotte Makhlouf and Brilliant Publications Limited

Radio Sunshine

A **contraction** is a word which has been shortened. The **apostrophe** tells us a letter or letters are missing. For example: 'I am' can be shortened to 'I'm'.

Doctor Gloom is very excited. Bobot the Robot has been asked to give a talk about himself on the radio. Can you shorten the underlined words so that his speech flows better?

I am called Bobot the Robot. This is my first radio interview so I am very excited. It is the first time I have done lots of talking. Doctor Gloom is pleased with my speech. There is a special computer for my voice. I have not done much talking until now. Doctor Gloom says he will programme me with lots of words so that I shall not find it difficult.

I am	I'm
we are	we're
they are	they're
how is	how's
it is	it's
there is	there's
cannot	can't
shall not	shan't
will not	won't

New controls are being put into Bobot the Robot to help him use more contractions when he is talking. Can you match the nuts and bolts together (the long form with its shortened form)?

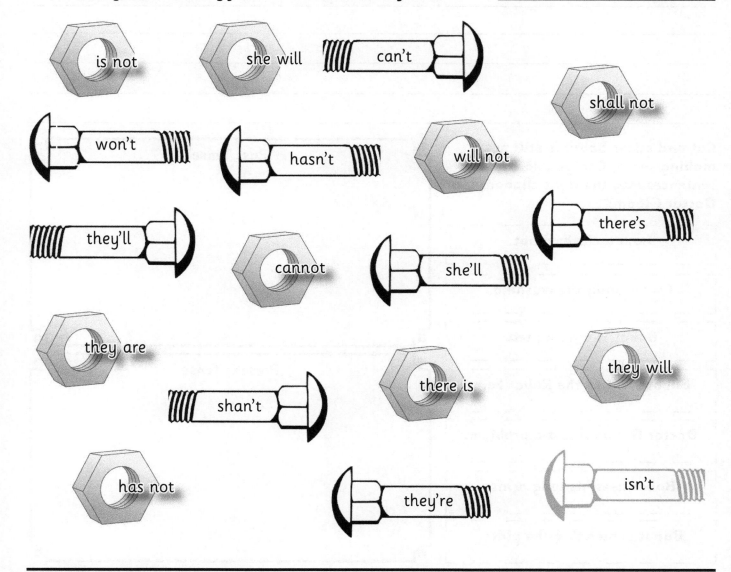

Bobot's Malfunction

Past tense is when an event has already happened. The present tense talks about something that is happening now.

Bobot the Robot has had a bit of a problem. His speech has suddenly gone wrong. He should be talking about something that has already happened – the past tense. Can you help Doctor Gloom fix the robot? Change the underlined words into past tense and then write it out neatly. The first has been done for you.

I ~~am~~ **was** walking to the computer. I **see**_____ Doctor Gloom in his laboratory. I **walk**_____ over to him. He **is**_____ pleased to see me. With him **is**_____ Professor Bloom. Professor Bloom **looks**_____ very serious. She **is**_____ wearing her special white coat. They **are**_____ talking about my feet. I **look**_____ down and **see**_____ that my feet **are**_____ blue! This **is**_____ very upsetting.

_____

_____

_____

_____

_____

Cut and stick! Bobot is still not making sense. Can you sort the sentences into the right clipboard for Doctor Gloom?

I am a clever robot.

I was doing the washing.

Bobot is making tea.

Bobot went to the Robot Fair.

Doctor Gloom found a problem.

Bobot uses his long arms.

Bobot is mending the plate.

Past Tense

Present Tense

Getting to Grips with English Grammar, Year 3
© Charlotte Makhlouf and Brilliant Publications Limited

Bobot's Speech

The **present perfect tense** is used when we talk about something that has happened at some time in the past. For example: I have travelled to France. OR He has been away on holiday.

Bobot is learning to use the present perfect when speaking. Colour the present perfect statements in orange.

Doctor Gloom is still trying to perfect Bobot's speech. Bobot needs to be able to use the present perfect tense. Sort the sentences into the correct part of Bobot's circuit board.

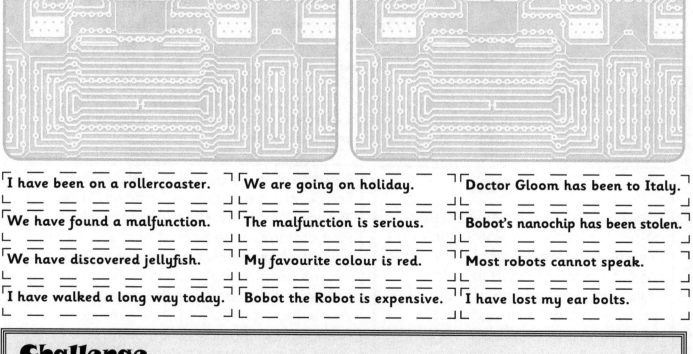

Present Perfect Tense

Other Statements

I have been on a rollercoaster.

We are going on holiday.

Doctor Gloom has been to Italy.

We have found a malfunction.

The malfunction is serious.

Bobot's nanochip has been stolen.

We have discovered jellyfish.

My favourite colour is red.

Most robots cannot speak.

I have walked a long way today.

Bobot the Robot is expensive.

I have lost my ear bolts.

Challenge

Imagine you are Bobot. Write six statements of your own to say what you can do using the present perfect tense. Put them in speech bubbles.

Spring Cleaning

Doctor Gloom has scattered his paperwork and notes everywhere. Help Bobot to pick up all the present perfect statements and put them in the rubbish bin.

> The **present perfect tense** is used when we talk about something that has happened at some time in the past. For example: I have travelled to France. OR He has been away on holiday.

> We have found a battery booster to charge Bobot quickly.

> We have walked a long way.

> Bobot has been targeted by evil Professor Spike!

> Bobot has short legs for a robot.

> They have given Bobot an award for being the best robot.

> Three factories want to use Bobot.

> The new robot will be a great success.

> Bobot has been my greatest invention.

> I have discovered the best way of keeping Bobot virus-free.

> Bobot is not affected by rust.

> Bobot does not want to be sent to other countries.

Challenge

Underline the present perfect sentences in this newspaper report. Then write at least four sentences of your own, in the present perfect, at the end of it.

Robot's Weekly

Bobot has been voted the best small domestic robot in the world. Doctor Gloom is very excited about the project. He has decided to build a more advanced version of Bobot. Projectorama will be investing £80 million to help Doctor Gloom. "We have realised that robots are very important," explained Crispin Nutter, Projectorama's Managing Director. "Bobot has been a great success," added Crispin Nutter. "Bobot is an inspiration to us all!" Projectorama have been delighted to share Doctor Gloom's new project. Doctor Gloom has not been available for comment. He has been on holiday with Bobot, taking a well-earned rest. Bobot will be going to Australia next month to show off his skills there. There has been a lot of excitement in Australia at Bobot's imminent arrival.

Getting to Grips with English Grammar, Year 3

Stop Press!

Bobot the Robot has been stolen by the evil Professor Spike. Can you finish off the news report about this terrible event? Use past tense to show events have already happened. Don't forget to draw a picture and add a caption!

Inventors Monthly

Bobot the Robot – Stolen

Bobot the Robot was stolen late last night from Doctor Gloom's laboratory. Local residents saw a black van parked outside at around 9.30pm.

_____

_____

_____

_____

_____

_____

_____

_____

_____

_____

_____

_____

_____

Vocabulary to help you

thieves

wanted

surprised

found

decided

police

searching

laboratory

evil plans

jealous

annoyed

frightened

witnesses

Challenge

Imagine that you are Bobot. Describe the events of the theft. Describe what happened, what you were doing at the time, how you felt, where you are …

Mini Quiz

Thankfully Bobot the Robot has been rescued from evil Professor Spike. Bobot has been talking to reporters.

Tick which sentences are punctuated correctly.

☐ "I was really frightened," said Bobot tearfully.

☐ Bobot told reporters, I thought I would never see Doctor Gloom again.

☐ "This was a horrible experience," sniffed Bobot.

☐ Doctor Gloom explained, "Bobot is a very special robot."

☐ I was so glad to get back home, explained Bobot.

Doctor Gloom has held a party to celebrate Bobot's return.

Correct the passage by putting in the missing speech marks.

The laboratory was covered in paper lanterns. It looks beautiful, exclaimed Professor Bloom happily. I am so glad Bobot was rescued, she continued. Bobot is a very special robot, said Professor Raven. You should receive a prize for him, he added kindly. Doctor Gloom made a speech to his friends. I don't like giving speeches, he told them shyly, but I am so grateful that Bobot has returned, I want to celebrate. Tony Brown raised his glass, to Bobot! he said. Welcome back! said everyone.

Colour the verbs (action words) blue.

jump	table	carry	cry	stir	beside	sing
sit	cat	mix	it	under	dance	Paris

Tick the sentences which show past tense.

☐ I went to Paris.   ☐ I am going to have a picnic.

☐ We flew to Spain yesterday.   ☐ He is having a lovely cold drink.

Getting to Grips with English Grammar, Year 3

Police Station Problems

Main clause
⇩

Subordinate clause. It tells you more about the doughnut.
⇩

Jerry ate his doughnut, <u>although there was hardly any jam in it!</u>

A. Underline all the subordinate clauses in the story below. The first has been done for you.

It is busy at the Police Station. PC Brown is having a well-earned break, <u>because there has been so</u> <u>much work to do.</u> Detective Donald has left lots of paperwork, as he is away on holiday. PC Brown has just found Mrs Woggle's dog, Tommy. Tommy is a lovely poodle, although he can be rather grumpy. PC Brown has arrested Toni Miller, who has been caught stealing watches from the jeweller. Soon PC Brown will be off to the zoo, where a large crocodile has gone missing. PC Brown is enjoying his tea break, even though all the biscuits have run out. PC Brown loves biscuits, especially the ones filled with chocolate and cream. He has a sweet tooth, which is very unhealthy for his teeth.

B. PC Brown has arrived at the zoo. It is not his favourite place because most of the creatures there are deadly! Professor Mei is giving him a tour of the zoo to help him work out what happened to the crocodile.

Can you write some interesting subordinate clauses, to describe things in more detail? The first has been done for you.

1. Dogsnout Birds have colourful wings, however their feet have poisonous feathers and sharp, deadly claws.

2. Lazlo, the crocodile, is huge because

_____ .

3. Lazlo was last seen by the ice-cream hut, although

_____ .

4. Lazlo likes visiting the Snotsnap dogs because

_____ .

5. Lazlo is not really dangerous, however

_____

Challenge

PC Brown has written a report about Lazlo's escape and what happened next at the zoo. Underline the subordinate clauses in PC Brown's report.

Three tourists saw Lazlo after he'd escaped, although it appeared they were too frightened to speak. There were claw marks by the gate, which had been left open! The crocodile's swamp smelt horrible, due to all the rubbish. I looked up frightened, as a screecher monkey howled. Mary, a girl who had orange plaits, saw Lazlo go towards the Snotsnap dogs. The Snotsnap dogs, who have runny noses, liked talking to Lazlo. Mrs Helga Higgins saw Lazlo at the car wash, which is very alarming!

Village Pet Show

PC Brown has been at the village Pet Show where there have been a few problems. Can you break down the following sentences into a main clause and a subordinate clause? The first has been done for you.

A **subordinate clause** tells you more about the main clause. Sometimes the **subordinate clause** can be in the middle of a sentence. For example: Dolly, the poodle with long ears, had fleas.

1. Bobby, the spaniel puppy, has dug up the flowers.

Subordinate clause
the spaniel puppy

Main clause
Bobby has dug up the flowers

2. Candy's rabbit ran away, because she was scared of the balloons.

Subordinate clause
_____

Main clause
_____

3. The black pony ate the buns, which made Mr Henry very angry.

Subordinate clause
_____

Main clause
_____

4. Meggie, who fell off her pony Twiggle, bought a large ice-cream.

Subordinate clause
_____

Main clause
_____

Challenge

Decide what is the main clause and what is the subordinate clause in each sentence. Write something suitable to finish the sentences.

Mrs Evans, with the poodle Brian, _____ .

The tea tent was empty because _____ .

Twiggle, who _____ , was a naughty pony.

The goats ate the sandwiches _____ .

I spoke to Mrs Ratty because _____ .

Getting to Grips with English Grammar, Year 3

PC Brown's Celebrity Mishaps

Life is never dull for PC Brown. He has been called to the Gogogo Club where some celebrities have had a few problems.

Cut and stick the most appropriate subordinate clause into the right boxes to give each sentence a main clause and a subordinate clause.

I was standing by the bar, [   ] , when the light fell on my head!

Baybella, [   ] , has lost her voice.

Frankie Donut slipped on a banana, [   ]

[   ] , Roy Butterball insisted on dancing wildly.

the famous singer	which made him sprain his ankle.
simply vanished into thin air.	Even though he had a broken leg
minding my own business	who has a bright, orange mane

Challenge

The celebrities have decided to leave the Gogogo Club early. They have each made up an excuse for leaving. Can you add a subordinate clause to each sentence to explain why.

Gupta Popadel the famous film star. "I must go now _____

_____ .

Dodge Chen the famous footballer. "I have to leave now _____

_____ .

Madge Gorm the film star. "I need to go _____

_____ .

PC Brown's Day Off

Prepositions show the relationship between a noun and other words in a sentence. They can tell you where something can be found.

PC Brown enjoys going fishing on his day off. Can you colour all the fish with prepositions of place in them?

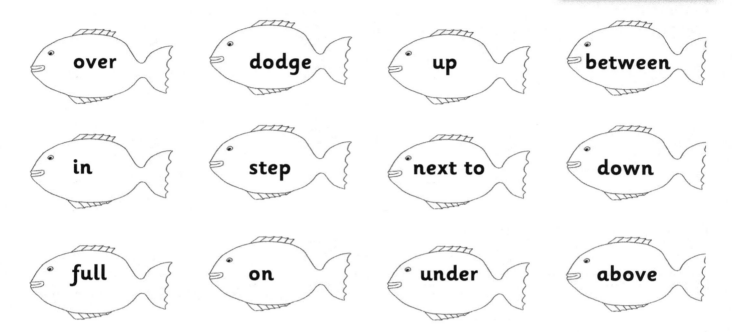

over   dodge   up   between

in   step   next to   down

full   on   under   above

Challenge

behind
below
between
above
in front of
over

Can you list some more prepositions here?

Say where the fish is in each picture, using the correct preposition from the box. The first has been done for you.

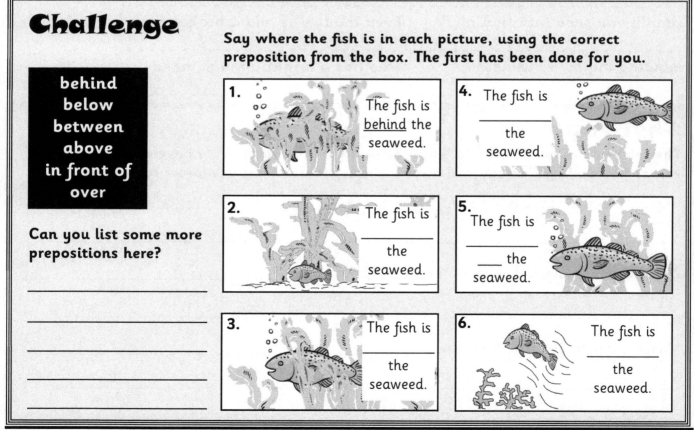

1. The fish is <u>behind</u> the seaweed.

4. The fish is ___ the seaweed.

2. The fish is ___ the seaweed.

5. The fish is ___ the seaweed.

3. The fish is ___ the seaweed.

6. The fish is ___ the seaweed.

Getting to Grips with English Grammar, Year 3
© Charlotte Makhlouf and Brilliant Publications Limited

Police Station Sort Out

The Police Station is in a bit of a muddle. Can you find PC Brown's things using the prepositions of place to help you?

His watch is _____ the books.

The biscuits are _____ the plate.

Could the files be _____ the shelf?

The telephone is _____ the computer.

The light is _____ the picture.

The picture is _____ the light.

The cat is _____ the table.

The table is _____ the cat.

Are his keys _____ the mug of tea?

in
on
under
below
above
beside
over

Challenge

Look at the picture below. Write a short story of your own to describe what is going on using as many prepositions of place as you can.

PC Brown's Reminders

Some **prepositions** tell you more about when something has happened, or is happening.

PC Brown can be rather forgetful. He has a board filled with reminders. Can you fill in the notes with one of the prepositions from the box? The first has been done for you.

<u>On</u> Tuesday you have a dental appointment.

_____ you leave for work, have a big breakfast.

PC Plod won't be back _____ 11.30am.

___ 3pm meet Detective Green.

___ Tuesday go to Poppleton Police Station.

At half _____ five I must feed the dog.

I must leave work _____ 5.30pm or I will miss my bus.

Remind Sally to post the letter _____ 12.00 or she will miss the post!

A few weeks' _____ , I went to Beech Hill School to talk to the children.

by
in
at
ago
until
past
on
before

Challenge

Mr Evans has left a message for PC Brown. Can you help him with his prepositions which he seems to have forgotten.

Dear PC Brown,
I am sorry to trouble you, but I was passing _____ and thought I would let you know about my missing cat, Oliver. When I got _____ from work yesterday, Oliver was not there. He often goes _____ to the cafe for some milk. But Mrs Jones ___ the cafe said he had not been ____! Some time _____, he was not home _____ very late. If you are driving _____ my house, perhaps you could pop ____ to see me.
Yours sincerely,
Mr Evans

Goblin Caves

PC Brown is looking for some missing pearls. He has been told they are in the Goblin Caves. Can you help him get through the caves safely. Find a word in the maze which is similar to those below and write it in the correct box.

| sad | _____ |

| happy |
| _____ |

| angry |
| _____ |

| eager | _____ |

| _____ | below |

| ugly | _____ |

| _____ | evil |

| hot |
| _____ |

| messy |
| _____ |

Start

horrible   under   untidy
keen   cross
joyful   stink   wicked
miserable   boiling

| smell | _____ |

Challenge

Find a good synonym for the following words, then make a little maze of your own to put them in.

| spiteful | fast | lovely |
| untidy | tiny | large |

At the Dentist

PC Brown has toothache, so he is visiting Dani the Dentist.

Cut and stick the correct synonym to match the words under the teeth. The first has been done for you.

junk	tall	neat
___	___	___

strange

odd

ill	angry	wet
___	___	___

tidy

sick

high

cross

rubbish

soaked

~~odd~~

PC Brown has been telling his friends about his experience at the dentist. Add a new synonym for the words underlined.

I was rather <u>frightened</u>_____ I can tell you. Dani is very <u>nice</u>_____. I had to sit in a <u>big</u>_____ chair. Dani <u>looked</u>_____ at my teeth carefully. I don't need any fillings! She then <u>cleaned</u>_____ my teeth for me. She had a <u>little</u>_____ spray which tickled. When she finished, she gave me a sticker for being <u>good</u>_____!

Challenge

Make some teeth of your own and put in some words. Ask a friend to see if they can find another word that means the same as the ones you have.

Jewellery Problems

Antonyms are words which mean the opposite of a word. For example:
hot – cold,
large – small.

Match the word in the jewel with its opposite.

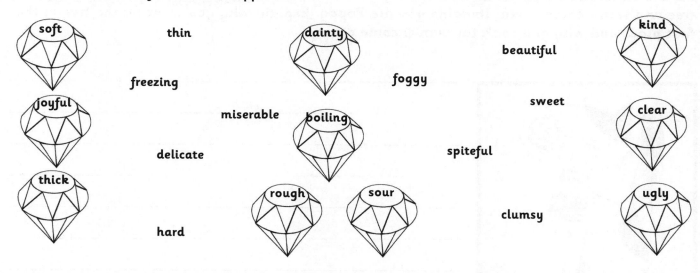

PC Brown has been asked to take a statement from some people who witnessed a robbery from the jewellery shop. Change the underlined words to ones which mean the opposite.

_____

_____

_____

_____

I saw Mrs Davis, the jeweller, <u>laughing</u> in front of her shop and <u>whispering</u> for help.

There was a man in a <u>white</u> coat, <u>walking</u> down the road very <u>slowly</u>.

_____

_____

When I <u>shut</u> the door, there were brooches and rings <u>neatly placed</u> all over the floor!

I was so <u>happy</u> when I saw the <u>tiny</u> man throwing a <u>small</u> sack on the table that I <u>stood up!</u>

_____

_____

Challenge

PC Brown has found a piece of paper on the floor which he thinks may be an important clue. It doesn't make sense. Can you help him by changing the underlined words into an appropriate antonym? See if you can then make a coded message of your own, using antonyms, for a friend to crack.

Put the jewels in the sack. Go to the <u>mended</u>, <u>new</u> bridge by the <u>straight</u> pier. There's a big café owned by Doris. She's a <u>horrible</u>, old woman who has a <u>black</u> cat called Chester. Give the jewels to her under cover of <u>daylight</u>. She is expecting you at <u>dawn</u>.

To the Rescue!

PC Brown has been called to Mrs Loop's garden. Her cat, Poppy, is stuck up her huge apple tree and won't come down. Imagine you are Poppy. Explain why you went up the tree in the first place and why you can't (or won't) come down.

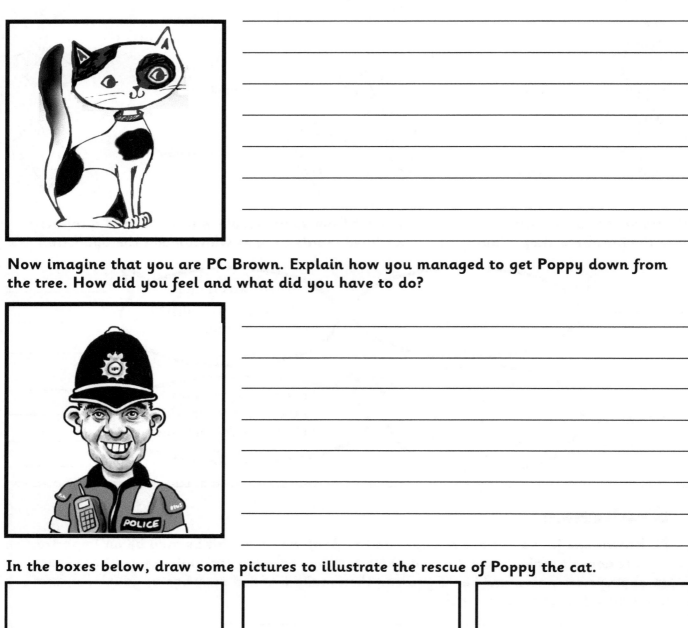

Now imagine that you are PC Brown. Explain how you managed to get Poppy down from the tree. How did you feel and what did you have to do?

In the boxes below, draw some pictures to illustrate the rescue of Poppy the cat.

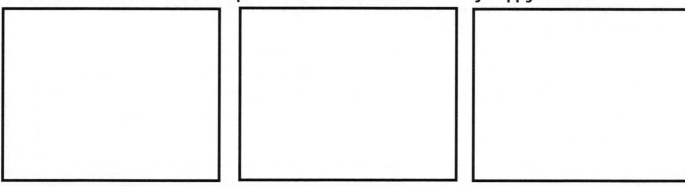

Getting to Grips with English Grammar, Year 3
© Charlotte Makhlouf and Brilliant Publications Limited

Mini Quiz

PC Brown often visits the children at Beech Hill School to tell them important information. In these sentences highlight the <u>main clause</u> red and the <u>subordinate clause</u> blue.

1. To cross the road safely, always look left and right.
2. Litter attracts wild animals, so pick it up and put it in a bin.
3. Make sure you wear a seat belt, as it could save your life.
4. The kitten, who was stuck up a tree, was ginger.
5. The dog, who was lost, found its owner.

Study the picture and write one of the prepositions from the box in each sentence.

1. The squirrel is jumping _____ a rock.

2. The cat is _____ the tree.

3. The kite is flying _____ the lady.

4. The bench is _____ the dog.

5. The hat is _____ the lady's head.

6. The kite is _____ in the sky.

| above |
| under |
| in |
| up |
| over |
| on |

PC Brown has been thinking about his day. Can you change the underlined word with another that means the same (synonym)?

| Slippery Sam is very <u>unkind</u>! | This has been a very <u>busy</u> day. | I would like a <u>hot</u> cup of tea. | I wonder if we might <u>catch</u> the jewellery thief! |

Write the correct prepositions from the box in the right sentence.

1. I am going to the zoo _____ I have been to the park.

2. _____ Friday I am going to the theatre.

3. I will be back at the station _____ it closes.

4. The cafe closes at _____ 6pm.

| before |
| around |
| after |
| on |

The Grand Opening!

Conjunctions are words which help to connect sentences. They can be used at the start of a sentence or in the middle of a sentence. They can help to express time or cause.

WELCOME!
Welcome to the Green Forest Holiday Park!
We hope you can come and stay with us **because** we have some of the best facilities and activities around!

RELAX!
Whenever you need peace and quiet, our woodland environment is the perfect place to be. **As soon as** you arrive, you will feel relaxed and at home.

ACCOMMODATION!
Choose to stay in a luxury Woodland Treehouse or Wilderness cabin for **as long as** you want. **By the time** you arrive, everything will be ready for you. **Once** you are settled, try out some of our fabulous activities.

ACTIVITIES
When you arrive you can start your activities. **After** a long woodland hike why not go swimming in our huge pool. Explore the forest on bikes **whenever** you like. **When** the sun sets, star watch from our treetop viewing gallery. **Before** you know it, you'll be ready for supper in our fabulous Lakeside Restaurant.

Did you notice all the words in bold? They are all conjunctions.

Challenge

Can you help to finish the story? Use an appropriate conjunction from the box.

THINGS TO DO

_____ a nice breakfast, why not head off to the lake. _____ you get there, take a canoe and go exploring. _____ you finish, you can go swimming or fishing. The lake is beautiful _____ you will find out! Stroll through the forest _____ it is time for lunch. _____ you are having lunch in the Squirrel Cafe, look out for wildlife. You can hire a bike for a _____. Why not ride around _____ it gets dark?

> after
> as
> as long as
> as soon as
> before
> by the time
> once
> since
> while
> until
> when
> whenever

Getting to Grips with English Grammar, Year 3

Treetop Walkway

The Tree Top Walkway is amazing. It is set high in the trees and you can explore parts of the forest along it. The Green Family have been asked to comment on the Tree Top Walkway. Can you add a suitable conjunction from the list to join their comments.

Conjunctions are words which help to connect sentences. They can be used at the start of a sentence or in the middle of a sentence. They can help to express time or cause.

I thought it was brilliant _____ I was a bit scared.

The view was beautiful _____ we were so high up.

I wanted to go round twice _____ Mum said no!

as
because
even though
until
but
since
consequently
as a result

Draw lines to match the endings with the correct beginnings.

The Tree Top Walkway is open all day	even though they ran away from us.
We took the wrong turning	but not at night.
We saw squirrels and deer	until we got to the lake and then we stopped.
We walked to the end	as a result we didn't get to the Tree Top Cafe.

Challenge

Granny and Grandad Green have also been on the Treetop Walkway even though Granny Green is terrified of heights. What do you think their comments might have been about the walkway. Can you write two comments for each of them? Don't forget to use conjunctions!

Holiday Park Rules

Because the Forest Holiday Park is set in a forest, they have some rules for their visitors to protect the wildlife. Write in the correct conjunctions.

Conjunctions to show cause.

Forest Walks
Please keep to the paths, _____ you might slip.

Our trees are ancient _____ please don't climb them.

Shoes should always be worn on the walkways _____ you do not hurt your feet.

_____ this is a conservation area, please do not chase or frighten the wildlife.

Conjunctions of cause

where
since
because
so
otherwise

Conjunctions to show time.

Bike Riding
_____ hiring your bike, get a map of the area so you don't get lost.

Barbecues are not allowed _____ they may start a forest fire.

Quad Biking
Fasten your helmet _____ you get on the bike.

Spa and Sauna
_____ you are relaxing, why not have a cool drink.

Conjunctions of time

after
as
as long as
as soon as
before
by the time
once
since
while
until
when

Challenge

Lenny is writing a small guest book to help visitors find their way around the Holiday Park. Can you help him finish it off using the correct conjunction?

We want you to have a happy stay _____ we value your custom. _____ you need help, please ask our staff for assistance. _____ our grand opening, we have just made a new spa. We have activities for adults _____ children.

since
because
so
whenever
and

Forest Park Activities

Adverbs are words which tell you how someone is saying something. For example:
Anna shouted angrily. 'Angrily' is the **adverb**.

Roger Browning is the Manager of the Forest Holiday Park. He is gathering comments from people who have tried some of the activities at the Holiday Park.

Add adverbs to the end of the sentences to show how the comments are being said.

"I loved the water slide!" giggled Benny
_____ .

"I had a beautiful walk," said Grandpa Green
_____ .

"The fishing was amazing!" squeaked Tilly
_____ .

"Four hours at the spa," sighed Mrs Lewis
_____ .

"I must admit I was frightened on the Treetop Walkway," whispered Granny Green
_____ .

"That bike ride was exhausting," muttered Harry
_____ .

"We saw deer!' shouted Eric
_____ .

Challenge

Underline all the adverbs you can find.

Dear Lazlo,
I am having a wonderful time at the Forest Holiday Park. I love swimming slowly in the big pool or playing archery carefully in the grounds. Chloe has played excitedly on the adventure playground, whilst I nearly died of fright on the Tree Top Walkway. I could hear other people shrieking excitedly on it but I had to get down quickly. It terrified me enormously! I danced energetically at the Tree Top Disco! Not everyone danced happily. I saw Mrs Green staring miserably at her glass. She looked unhappily at the dancers which was a shame. I do wish you were here with me.
Much love
Peggy xxx

List them all here. Then see if you can use them in sentences of your own.
_____
_____
_____
_____
_____
_____
_____
_____

At the Reception Desk

Adverbs can tell you more about a verb. For example: Teddy shouted angrily. 'Angrily' is the **adverb**, it tells you how Teddy shouted.

Tina, at the reception desk, is very busy. A lot of people want to book some new activities at the Forest Holiday Park.

How do you think these people might be saying or asking their statements?

"I was really hoping for three tickets," moaned Alfie _____.

"There's a new water slide!" shouted Dilly _____.

Sally sobbed _____ "but I wanted to see the beach!"

"Four tickets for the Salsa Show!" announced Derek _____.

"I can't believe there are no bikes left!" exclaimed Mrs Flagg _____.

"Oh no!" squeaked May _____, "I've dropped my sunglasses!"

Look at the adverb and then write what you think Tina might be saying.

" _____," snapped Tina crossly.

" _____," began Tina quickly.

" _____," said Tina patiently.

" _____," announced Tina calmly.

Challenge

Tina has to deal with a lot of tricky people at the Forest Holiday Park. Use each of the adverbs in the box and write sentences to show what you think Tina might be saying to or thinking of one of the tricky people.

sweetly
crossly
kindly
nervously

Theatre Production

Dillcombe Bay Theatrical Company are doing a play. Unfortunately, they are experiencing a few problems backstage. Some of the props have gone missing! Use the adverbs in the box to modify the adjectives.

This is _____ disgraceful!

Everyone is _____ worried about their things.

Gareth, the show's Director, is _____ furious about the missing props.

This is a _____ difficult situation!

"This is all _____ distressing," moaned Gareth.

really
very
absolutely
terribly
extremely
understandably

Underline the modifying adverbs in these short conversations.

1. Melba Coast is missing her fan for Act II.
   "This is absolutely disgraceful," she shouted. "I am terribly upset."

2. Colin Crumble is missing his gloves for Scene 3.
   "This is extremely inconvenient," Colin grumbled, "I am very annoyed!"

3. Tamsin Thwistle has lost her hat for Scene 1.
   "This is really annoying!"

4. "I know you are all understandably cross," began Gareth.

Challenge

Can you find all the adverbs from the box below in this passage? Some of the adverbs modify the verbs and some of them modify the adjectives. The first two have been done for you.

"Look everyone," began Gareth <u>calmly</u>. "I know you're <u>really</u> upset, but we will find the props." Melba Coast began grumbling unhappily. "This is terribly annoying," she snapped crossly. "I don't need my hat," said Tamsin quickly. "I can do without it." In the dressing room, Mrs Evans was crying noisily. "This is extremely bad," she sniffed miserably. "They all blame me! Of course I'm understandably upset." Crispin Crust has been searching furiously for his parchment letter. He is extremely cross. "I'm really desperate for that letter," he shouted nastily. Gareth is speaking quickly to Dorian Whisp, the stage manager, who is terribly worried. "We can't do the sword fight without the swords," he explained miserably.

Dillcombe Bay

Some **adverbs** can tell us WHEN things happened. They are called **adverbs of time**.

Forest Holiday Park is not far from beautiful Dillcombe Bay. Dillcombe Bay is famous for its beaches and dinosaur fossils. Old Reg, the Fisherman, has lived at Dillcombe Bay for 45 years. He has lots of stories to tell.

Can you fill in the missing adverbs of time into old Reg's account of smuggling and fossil hunting? Use the words in the box below to help you.

as soon as	when	since	before	whenever	once

Dillcombe Bay Smugglers

_____ I was born, there used to be smugglers along this coast. _____ there was no moon they would head for shore. _____ it was dark, they would land their goods. _____ ashore, the cargo was usually hidden away in caves or caverns. _____ I walk along the beach I think about the old smugglers! But _____ then, no smugglers have been spotted in this area.

Fossil Hunts

_____ we can, we hold fossil hunts along the beach. _____ there used to be dinosaurs here! _____ then, we have always looked for fossils. _____ the tide goes out, you can start hunting! _____ I find a fossil, I get very excited. _____ I hunt for fossils, my wife fishes in the sea. _____ a long day fossil hunting, we return home!

after	once	since	whenever	as soon as	while	when

Imagine you have been on a fossil hunt with old Reg. Describe your day, using the adverbs of time from the box, in a postcard to a friend.

after	once
by the time	when
as soon as	while
before	

_____

_____

_____

_____

_____

_____

_____

_____

At the Water Park

Some **adverbs** can tell us WHEN things happened. They are called **adverbs of time**.

The Forest Holiday Park has a fabulous water park. Roger, the Manager, is trying to produce a poster to remind people how to behave when they are at the water park.

Can you help him put in some important adverbs of time? Draw a picture for each rule.

| as soon as | when | since | before | whenever | once |

Water Park Rules
Welcome to the Forest Holiday Park Water Park!

_____ using the mega slide, please listen to the safety instructions.

_____ you have been down the slide, please move out of the way quickly.

_____ the slide is clear, you may go down.

_____ swimming, please take a shower.

_____ the whistle blows, please listen to the lifeguard.

Challenge

Roger needs to make another poster to remind people to be safe on the beach. Working with a friend, can you produce a poster using some <u>adverbs of time</u>, to remind people of the rules at the beach? Brainstorm your ideas first of all on paper and then draw your poster.

At the Beach

Adverbs of cause tell us WHAT has happened as a result of an event. For example: <u>Because</u> he fell off his bike, Ray broke his leg. This tells us the cause.

Roger has been called down to the beach where there have been a few problems. Lenny the Lifeguard has been explaining the problems to him on his walkie talkie.

Highlight the <u>adverb of cause</u> in red. Explain what effect this cause has created. The first has been done for you.

as	because	<u>now that</u>	since	consequently
thus		therefore		however

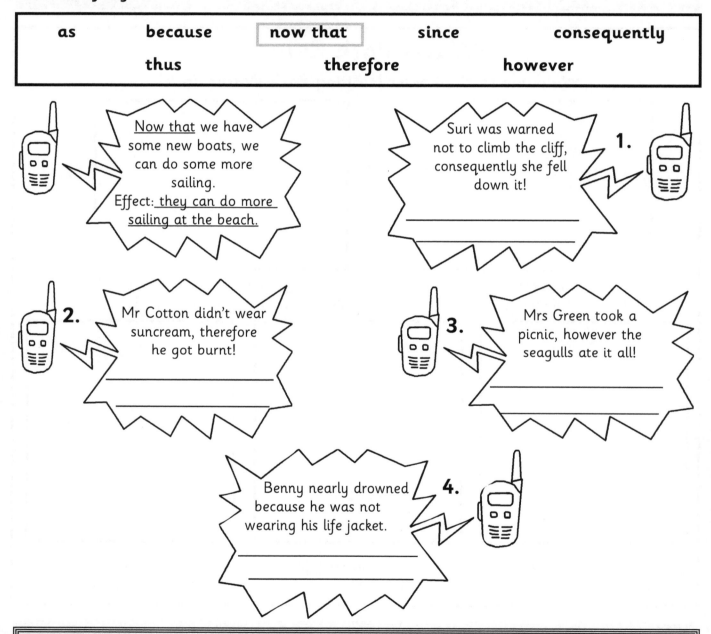

<u>Now that</u> we have some new boats, we can do some more sailing.
Effect: <u>they can do more sailing at the beach.</u>

1. Suri was warned not to climb the cliff, consequently she fell down it!

_____

2. Mr Cotton didn't wear suncream, therefore he got burnt!

_____

3. Mrs Green took a picnic, however the seagulls ate it all!

_____

4. Benny nearly drowned because he was not wearing his life jacket.

_____

Challenge

Imagine you are Lenny the Lifeguard. Think of four more problems which could occur on the beach. Use suitable adverbs of cause from the box above.

Getting to Grips with English Grammar, Year 3

New Fossil Discovered

Little Charlie Dimble has been climbing (he should not have been!) on the cliffs of Dillcombe Bay. As a result, he has found a new fossil! A reporter from the Dillcombe Bay Daily Newspaper is reporting the event.

Imagine you are the reporter and write an article for the paper. Use some of the ideas in the box to help you with your writing. Be imaginative! Don't forget to draw a picture.

Dillcombe Bay Daily News
Large Fossil Discovered

- the fossil is huge
- might be a new dinosaur
- Charlie was half way up the cliff
- Charlie slipped
- earth slid away
- Charlie is 8
- fossil found in the early morning

Remember to use your 5 'W's when writing.

WHO
WHAT
WHY
WHEN
WHERE

Use past tense!

Challenge

Imagine you are Charlie's Mother. You are giving an interview to the reporter from the Dillcombe Bay Daily Newspaper. Describe how you feel about Charlie's discovery and the events that led up to it. You could record your interview with a friend then write it up neatly.

Mini Quiz

Read the passage and fill in a suitable conjunction from the box.

The Forest Cabin

Choose to stay in a forest cabin

_____ it is fun to be in the forest.

_____ they are set in the woods,

they are not far from the main building.

Forest Cabins are great for families

_____ they are nice and big!

as
because
even though
until
but
since
consequently
as a result

The Tree Top House

_____ they are high up, the

steps are easy to climb. Great for couples

_____ they are small. Watch the

wildlife on the lake _____ the sun

goes down. They are not suitable for

small children _____ they are good for

teenagers!

Woodland Pod Dwelling

Our visitors wanted to be close to the wildlife. _____

we designed the Woodland Pod! _____ it looks small, it has

lots of room inside. There is a kitchen, a bathroom _____ no

television!

Choose four adverbs from the box and use them in a sentence of your own about the Forest Holiday Park.

1. _____

2. _____

3. _____

4. _____

as soon as
when
since
before
whenever
once

Getting to Grips with English Grammar, Year 3

Trouble in Giantville

Read the newspaper report below and highlight all the words in the passage that you did not know the meaning of. Use a dictionary to find out what they mean.

Giant's Weekly

Monday 7th October

Troll Trouble

Giants in Giantville were angry last night, when more rude messages appeared on house and garden walls.

This is the eighth case of nasty comments and rude words which have been appearing all over homes and gardens in Giantville, leaving resident giants angry and upset.

Trolls were spotted on the High Street.

The Giant Police believe that local trolls from the woods are writing the messages, as two trolls were spotted last night, running towards the woods. The trolls were holding cans of red paint and brushes and had been spotted near a freshly painted wall earlier in the evening. "It's hard to catch them," Constable Crinkle told reporters, "because they are so quick and cunning."

"It is very upsetting," Giantess Grinkle told reporters. "We giants are peaceful creatures and these rude messages are hurtful, unkind and unnecessary. Cleaning up afterwards also takes ages and is very expensive!"

Mayor Giant Grumble has warned everyone in Giantville not to do anything to retaliate.

Troll spotted!

"We don't want to make the situation worse by hurting the trolls," he told giants at a meeting in the Town Hall.

Giantville is a peaceful place, where the giants are proud of their homes and gardens. It is believed that the trolls are jealous of the giants and are trying to cause trouble between them to begin a Fourth Troll War.

"Trolls enjoy fighting," Giant Gogg, an expert in troll habits, told reporters. "They love making weapons and fighting but they live underground and they miss the sun and fresh air at times."

Whilst the giants do a big clean up, Councillors are planning to meet to discuss what they can do to end this situation, which is fast becoming a real headache for everyone in Giantville.

Challenge

Newspapers have special features. Can you design a new headline for this article which is punchy and captivating? Can you also design a new picture?

Newspaper Features

Newspapers have specific features. They need the name of the paper (Giant's Weekly). They need a headline for the main story. They need the day's date, a photograph or picture for the main story and a caption for the main photograph or picture. There is then the main story. Read the very short stories below and make up a punchy headline for them. Draw a picture for the story and give it an appropriate caption.

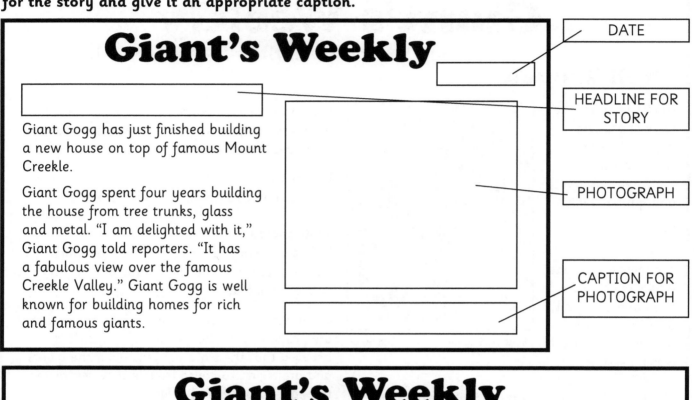

Giant's Weekly

DATE

HEADLINE FOR STORY

PHOTOGRAPH

CAPTION FOR PHOTOGRAPH

Giant Gogg has just finished building a new house on top of famous Mount Creekle.

Giant Gogg spent four years building the house from tree trunks, glass and metal. "I am delighted with it," Giant Gogg told reporters. "It has a fabulous view over the famous Creekle Valley." Giant Gogg is well known for building homes for rich and famous giants.

Giant's Weekly

Giantess Glush has been put in prison having accidentally squashed an entire human village last night.

Giantess Gush was on her way back from a party at Giant Gweek's house when she lost her way in the darkness and accidentally stepped on the little village of Dipple. "I had dropped my glasses," Giantess Glush sobbed to reporters, "so I couldn't see … ."

Challenge   Can you finish the article about Giantess Glush?

Getting to Grips with English Grammar, Year 3

Fashion Feature

Paragraphs help to separate information in a piece of writing. They should start on a new line and they should be indented.

Giantess Grizzle has designed a new range of clothing for giants. She has written an article for the newspaper.

Can you separate her information into paragraphs for her? Use a highlighter pen to show where the new paragraphs will be and then write it out carefully below. The first paragraph has been done for you.

I am thrilled to show you my beautiful new range of clothing for giants. I have been designing the range of clothing for the last two years in my mountain top studio. I have used spiders as my inspiration because they spin such lovely, delicate, yet strong webs. I want my clothes to look delicate and beautiful too as well as be strong enough for tough giant use. My latest collection features some pretty swim wear, some beautiful day wear, as well as some ballgowns and suits for men. My next collection will be focusing on clothing for work.

I am thrilled to show you my beautiful new range of clothing for giants. I have been designing the range of clothing for the last two years in my mountain top studio.

_____

_____

_____

_____

_____

_____

_____

_____

Challenge

If you could add two new paragraphs to Giantess Grizzle's feature, what would you write? Add them to your passage above.

Giant's Weekly: Letters

The Editor in Chief of Giant's Weekly receives many letters from local giants and sometimes trolls. The Editor has to reply to some of these letters. Letters need paragraphs too. Use a red pen to show where the paragraphs should be in these letters. The first paragraph has been indented for you.

Dear Giantess Gringle,

Thank you for your letter about the recent troll situation. Many of my friends are trolls and they are very sad about the latest troll troubles. We are hoping to hold a small fireworks party next week to celebrate the harvest festival, to which all trolls and giants are invited. We hold a fireworks party every year so we hope that you can come. On another note, were you aware that there are a lot of trolls who are trying to gather together to discuss the troubles. They want to meet at the Grym Hotel next week. We hope you can be there too.

With Best Wishes

Giant Groan

Dear Grimbal,

We were very interested to hear about your recent adventures in the Greenhorn Mountains. It is exciting to hear that there are Cookweed birds living there. I have written to the head of the Cookweed Society who is planning to send an expert to the Mountains. He would be pleased to meet you there. This is an exciting find and we would love you to write an article for the Giant's Weekly paper all about the Cookweed birds you have discovered. I look forward to hearing from you.

With Best Wishes

Giant Groan

Challenge

Imagine you are the Editor in Chief, Giant Groan. Write a letter to Giantess Twinkle telling her all about the troll troubles. Use Giant Groan's notes below to help you. Try to write at least three paragraphs for your letter. Don't forget to end it correctly.

- Rude writing on walls, vandalised gardens, things stolen from sheds
- Giant Police have set up roadblocks and are patrolling the town
- Possible Fourth Troll War
- Local giants are worried
- Having a fireworks party to celebrate harvest and bring trolls and giants together
- Shopkeepers have boarded up shops
- Some trolls were caught stealing garden equipment.

Under the Mountain

Giant Gogg has written a Guidebook on Trolls. He has just added some new information to his book, only he has forgotten to put in all his paragraphs. Can you highlight where the paragraphs should be then write the passage out neatly using paragraphs?

Trolls are known for being fierce and warlike. However, there are some trolls who live a peaceful life under the mountains. These trolls enjoy making beautiful jewellery and carving pictures into their walls. Most trolls have quick tempers and jump into fights without thinking. Their swords are sharp and deadly and they learn to fight from a young age. Troll children go to school from the age of five where they learn to read and write and compose songs.

Challenge

Write two paragraphs giving information about what trolls like to eat. You can make up the information and be imaginative.

Write two paragraphs on what trolls like to do in their free time. Again, be imaginative. You can make up the information.

All About Giantville

Headings and **subheadings**, help to present information neatly.

Headings

What heading might you give these pieces of writing? Read them carefully and decide what the main theme is all about. Then give it a heading.

___ ___ ___ ___ ___ ___ ___ ___

Giantville is the oldest town in Giantania. It overlooks the beautiful Minkle Mountain range and Dewdrop Valley. It has a population of over 60 giants, who live peacefully as farmers, teachers and designers.

___ ___ ___ ___ ___ ___ ___ ___

Giant Gruff is Giantville's baker. He has been baking bread for the town for the last twenty years. He makes all kinds of rolls, loaves and pastries. Giant Gruff loves icing and decorating his pastries!

Headings and Subheadings

Headings tell you what the whole piece of writing is about. Subheadings give you more information about a small part of that writing. For example:

Trolls

It is under the Minkle Mountains that the trolls live. The trolls have been living there for thousands of years. They have carved out a whole city under the mountains and will not let outsiders in.

<u>Troll Homes</u>

The trolls have carved out small homes in which they live with all their family. They have been carved out of the rock.

The **heading** is 'Trolls'.

The **subheading** is 'Troll Homes'.

Challenge

Can you write some information under the heading of TEETH. Then write some more information under the subheading of 'Going to the Dentist'.

Teeth

_____

_____

_____

Going to the Dentist

_____

_____

_____

Getting to Grips with English Grammar, Year 3

All About Giantville

> **Headings** and **subheadings**, help to present information neatly.

Give this piece of writing a heading. Then give it two subheadings.

——— ——— ——— ——— ——— ———

Giant Gryn lives in Giantville. He has been living there for many years and is a celebrity because of his garden. Giant Gryn is not the only celebrity; Giant Gwin, the celebrated writer, also lives there in a large mansion outside the town.

——— ——— ——— ——— ——— ———

Giant Gwin started writing books when she was very young. She loves animals and she has three giant cats called Grog, Grigg and Grin. Giant Gwin has just written an exciting adventure story about a giant caught in a terrible storm on Mount Gloom.

——— ——— ——— ——— ——— ———

Giantville has many beautiful gardens. Most giants love gardening and keep both plants and vegetables. They adore pottering around their gardens and holding garden parties for their friends.

Challenge Can you write some interesting information about Giant Homes.

Giant Homes

Mountain Homes

Lakeside Homes

The Giant's Express Newspaper

Giantess Fleur has copied some sentences from her local newspaper. Cut them out and sort them into the correct box.

Exclamations

Commands

Questions

Statements

There will be a day of celebration.

WATCH OUT!

Why did you do it?

Riots in Giantville reach third day!

2 MILLION YEAR OLD GIANT SKELETON FOUND!

It is believed that the two giants were not guilty.

Did you take the flowers?

The young giant said it was a foolish thing to do.

Put the rubbish in the bin.

This is a good day for all giants.

Local giant in avalanche horror!

Take the watering can to the shed.

Write four sentences of your own and put them into the correct box. Don't forget, they should be suitable for The Giant Express!

Challenge

Take two of the statements from above and try to write the whole article from where they were taken.

The Miracle of Giantville

Proofreading means checking your work to see that it makes sense and there are no grammatical or punctuation errors.

Giant Grog has been writing an article about the Miracle of Giantville. He has become rather carried away and has made a lot of mistakes. Can you find the mistakes and correct them for him? There are quite a few! Look for missing capital letters, full stops and speech marks! He may have misspelt a few words too! Use a highlighter to mark the mistakes and then write it out neatly and correctly. The first has been done for you.

What's Missing?

! ? , . " "

The ~~Mira~~kle of Giantville
(Miracle)

Do you believe in miracles? Won dark night a young giantess calld Gwinda was lost in the fourest she had no idea were she was. all of a sudden she thawght she felt gentle hands pushing her away she was so tired, she fell asleep against a tree in the morning she realised she was literally a few feet away from a terrible clyff! I cud have fallen down it, she said, if it hadnt been for those strange hands pushing me. It was a miracle i built my home not far from the cliff and called it grimlock. Other giants came and settled here two and so giantville was born.

Giant Greevy has been doing the advertisements for the next issue of Giant's Weekly. He hasn't checked his work either. Can you proofread his work for him and correct it?

Win a holiday

Wyn a holiday to the Giantania Coast. Swym with dolfins and go fishing on the see. This is a grate opportunity to relax and recharge yor batterys. Text: GIANTWIN23 to GIANT HOLIDAYS.

Giant ice-cream

Fabulous Flavours is a new ice-creem shopp for giants in giantville. choose from a variety of new and exciting flayvors. why not try gooseberri deelight or lavender and ginger creem. Try our fabulous flavours?

Challenge:

Can you make an advertisement of your own for Giant's Weekly? Decide on a product (food, gardening products, vehicles, DIY, sports equipment, for example). Then think of something wonderful to advertise, for example: food – giant doughnuts.

Trolls Wanted

Adjectives are describing words. They can tell you what people, places and things look like. For example: A beautiful, red squirrel.

The Giant Police have put up 'Wanted' posters to search for the troublesome trolls. Descriptions of them are all over the town. Highlight the adjectives in yellow!

WANTED For Smash and Grab

A small, red-faced troll with bright orange hair was spotted raiding a garden shed. The troll is believed to have big hands and pointed ears. He was wearing a brown jacket, red-checked shirt, blue trousers and big, heavy black boots. Last seen carrying a cream-coloured, canvas sack believed to be filled with garden tools.

WANTED!

A short, black-haired troll, wearing a green and red spotted dress and blue boots. The troll was seen carrying two beautiful, yellow Sneakle Roses in her arms whilst on her back she had a black rucksack filled with small garden tools.
REWARD: 25 gold pieces

Challenge:

Draw a troll. Make a list of all the adjectives you would use to describe them. Then make a wanted poster of your own using all your adjectives.

My Troll

My Adjectives

Getting to Grips with English Grammar, Year 3

At the Garden Centre

Giant's Weekly are doing a big feature on the new Giantville Garden Centre. Giantella has been organising all the labels for the special plants on show. She is trying to use plenty of interesting adjectives to describe them. Can you help her?

Underline the adjectives in these labels in green.

This beautiful, majestic Loopal Plant will be a wonderful addition to your garden. It loves cool, shady places and a little bit of bright sunlight.

Take home a gorgeous, fluffy Weeping Whistle Bush. Its sweet singing will echo around your garden. In Summer, they bear tiny, orange berries which can be crushed to make a delicious, tangy jam.

See if you can write a label of your own for these strange plants. Use plenty of adjectives to describe them.

Googaloo Whistler Fern

_____
_____
_____
_____
_____
_____

Purple Snap-finger-snacker

_____
_____
_____
_____
_____

Snooper-looper Flower

_____
_____
_____
_____
_____

Challenge

The Garden Centre has some exciting areas for enthusiastic gardeners to explore, with amazing plants in them to buy: the new Aquatic area, Mountain Plants area, a fabulous Guard Plants area (they guard your garden) and a Soft and Scented Section. Imagine you are Giantella. Make a big poster for each area (or just choose one area) and, using plenty of adjectives, describe what it looks like and what the plants are like. Draw pictures of the plants and arrange your information attractively so giants will want to visit!

Troll Troubles Worsen

Similes compare things to one another using the words 'as' or 'like'. For example: as cold as ice, as green as grass.

Can you find all the similes in the newspaper report? Highlight them with your favourite highlighter when you find them. How many paragraphs were used?

Giant's Weekly

12th April 3087

Troll Troubles Worsen

The troll crisis increased last night as a group of trolls went as mad as monkeys in Giantville, setting fire to sheds and looting shops.

Local giants were alarmed as eight trolls ran rampage around the town screaming like banshees, breaking shop windows, looting and setting fire to garden sheds. "I watched them saunter into town as cool as cucumbers," Giant Goff told reporters. "They charged into my garden as bold as brass and set fire to my shed! I was as mad as a hatter!"

Mayor Grumble helped the Giant Police to get the trolls out of town. "They were screaming and yelling, their eyes as black as coal," explained Mayor Grumble. "They smirked at us looking as pleased as punch as they broke two shop windows. PC Giant Greebly stood as strong as an oak and roared at them to leave."

Trolls are known to be difficult creatures. One minute they look as sweet as pie, the next minute they look as mean as snakes.

At least eight trolls rampaged through the town last night.

After a night of worry and watching the trolls like hawks, the Giantville Police were finally able to get rid of them. A 24 hour watch has been put in place and road blocks have been set up to protect Giantville.

Normally as gentle as lambs, the giants are now angry and want justice.

Challenge

Imagine you are PC Giant Greebly. Describe your encounter with the trolls. See how many of these similes you can use within your writing: as large as life, as sweet as pie, as hard as nails, exploded like a volcano, as angry as a lion. For a super challenge you could make up some similes of your own to add to your writing!

Troll Talk

In their underground caverns, the trolls are thinking about and discussing the latest outbreak of troubles up in Giantville. Identify the simile in each speech bubble and underline it.

1. This is getting silly. They are as mad as hatters to keep fighting!

2. They strolled into those gardens, as cool as cucumbers! I was so shocked!

3. I wish this nonsense would stop. They are fighting like cats and dogs for no reason!

4. Billy said Noggin was as hard as nails – he wants to avenge all the trolls!

5. Like a dog with a bone is Old Noggin! He should go home and stop being so silly!

6. It makes me feel as cold as ice just to think of it.

See if you can make up a simile of your own. The first has been done for you.

As slippery as <u>glass</u>.	As sweet as _____ .	As soft as _____ .
As pretty as _____ .	As clever as _____ .	As fiery as _____ .
As cheeky as a _____-___ .	As smooth as a _____ .	

Challenge

See if you can use some of the new similes you have made above in some Troll Talk of your own. What do you think the trolls could be saying to one another?

Giants at Home Magazine

Metaphors compare different things. They suggest that two things are the same but they never use the words 'as' or 'like'. For example: 'The lamp was a beacon of hope' OR 'The sun is a fiery furnace'.

Can you find all the metaphors in the Giants at Home article? Underline them in green.

Giants at Home

Back from climbing Mount Gloom, Giantess Glenda talks to Giants at Home Magazine.

Looking more relaxed than a cat, Giantess Glenda is happy to be back home in Giantville. "Mount Gloom was a journey of discovery for me," she told Giant Gwin from 'Giants at Home'. "It was hugely dangerous. I had to outrun an avalanche faster than lightning," she recalls. "Normally I am at home but this trip was a breath of fresh air for me."

Giantess Glenda has spent months preparing for her climb. On Mount Gloom, the snow was a white blanket. "It was incredibly deep, at night the wind was an angry witch. I would look up at the sky where the stars were sparkling diamonds. It was magical."

Challenge

Can you invent some metaphors of your own for this article in Giants at Home? Draw a picture in the box for the article.

Giant Goffin has gone on an exciting adventure to find the Valley of Diamonds. With him is his friend Giant Gruff. Here is his account.

"The river was a _____ _____, so it was dangerous to cross. Giant Gruff was _____ _____ as he carried our luggage across. My pulse was _____ _____ as we saw the Valley of

Diamonds. My eyes were _____ _____ as I climbed towards it. Behind us the wind was _____ _____."

The Troll Times

Can you write a newspaper article for The Troll Times giving exciting details about the glorious raids they have been having on Giantville? Don't forget to set out the paper carefully with a punchy, exciting headline, a picture and a caption for the picture. Don't forget your paragraphs!

The Troll Times

(Date)

(Heading)

(Picture)

(Caption for picture)

Challenge

Can you design some advertisements for the newspaper – make sure that they are appropriate for trolls!

Mini Quiz

A. Put in the correct punctuation. Write beside the sentence whether it is a question, a statement, a command or an exclamation.

This is amazing ___	
Are you coming to Giantville ___	
This has been a difficult time for the giants ___	
Did you buy me a Giant's Weekly ___	
Stop that ___	
Get out of Giantville ___	

? !

.

? !

B. Mayor Giant Grumble has written a short statement. Draw lines to show where a paragraph should start.

Fellow giants, we must try to stay calm in the middle of this crisis. Please stay inside your homes at night time and do not go out unless you have to. Constable Crinkle has told me that the Giant Police will be patrolling Giantville day and night. He has also set up road blocks to stop the trolls getting in. Giants with families outside Giantville are urged not to visit unless it is necessary. Families should talk to one another by telephone.

C. Cut out and stick the similes and metaphors into the correct boxes.

Metaphors	Similes

As quick as lightning, he pounced.

The wind was an angry witch.

The sun was a burning light.

His eyes were as hard as nails.

Her heart was as cold as ice.

Her eyes were shining stars.

Answers

Giant Gryn's Garden *Page 13*
Gobbler Fungi: medicine, medicinal, medical, paramedics.
Mrs Grizzlekin: help, helpful, forgive, forgiven.
Bat Cave: headache, head torch, headgear, head, heading, headed.

Challenge: Play: played, playing, playful, replay, player
Real: unreal, realistic, reality, really, realise
Happy: unhappy, happiness, happier
Sign: resign, signing, signed, resigned, redesign, designer, signature, signpost, signal.

Frugal Berry Theft *Page 14*
Managing, mismanage, manage, manager.
Rebake, baked, bake, bakery, baker.
Flowered, flowery, flower.

Challenge: Love: loved, lovely, loveless, unloved, loving, lover.
Port: import, report, reporter, reporting, export, transport, transporter, support, supportive.
Take: retake, taking, mistake.
Joy: joyful, enjoy, joyous.
Cook: cooked, uncooked, recook, cooker, cookery, cooking.
Wrap: wrapped, unwrapped, wrapping, rewrap, wrapper.

Plant Sort *Page 15*
Word families: help, helper, helped, helpful, helpless, unhelpful.
Covering, cover, coverage, recover, uncover, rediscover.
Medic, medically, medicinal, medicine.
Underwrite, rewrite, writer, written, write.
Triangle, tricycle, tripod.

Challenge: The two words families are 'photo' and 'invent'. The odd words out are invantage and disvents.

In the Potting Shed *Page 16*
Do not let the dog <u>bury</u> its bone!
<u>Meet</u> Giantess Gwenda at the post office.
Water the small, pink <u>flower</u> by the pond.
Repair the <u>hole</u> in the shed roof.
Clean the 3-piece <u>suite</u> in the lounge.
Look for Niki's teddy <u>bear</u> in the garden.
Buy <u>plain</u> buns for the picnic.
There has been no <u>rain</u> to water the plants.

Challenge: Written this day in the <u>reign</u> of Good Queen Bessie, may peace be upon her <u>soul</u>. '<u>For</u> <u>I</u>, Giant Thickbeard the <u>Great</u> leave to the finder of this parchment, some treasure! <u>I</u> have sailed around the <u>world</u> and <u>seen</u> such <u>sights</u> though the

<u>weather</u> has often <u>been</u> poor. Giant waves, the <u>sight</u> of <u>which</u> <u>would</u> make a <u>grown</u> <u>male</u> shake. You will find the treasure under the old oak…

Jabberjoot Leaves *Page 17*
hear – mishear
trust – mistrust or distrust
clear – unclear
take – mistake
miss – dismiss
active – inactive
polite – impolite
legal – illegal

Challenge: faithful – unfaithful; justice – injustice; patient – impatient; helpful – unhelpful; possible – impossible; adequate – inadequate; may – dismay; comfortable – uncomfortable; balance – imbalance.

At the Garden Centre *Page 18*
Super: superman, superglue, superhero, superpower, superstar.
Anti: antifreeze, antidote, antiseptic, antibiotic.
Auto: autopilot, automate, automobile.

Challenge: Sentences and choice of words will vary.

In the Garden *Page 19–20*
<u>a</u> dragonfly, <u>a</u> pond, <u>a</u> butterfly, <u>an</u> ant, <u>a</u> Creekle tree, <u>an</u> apple tree, <u>a</u> deck chair, <u>an</u> egg, <u>an</u> iguana, <u>a</u> leaf, <u>an</u> Oogle bird, <u>an</u> olive bush, <u>a</u> winkle fish, <u>a</u> tractor, <u>a</u> compost heap.
Dear Councillor Chuff,
I think Giant Gryn's garden should be shut down! It is **a** dangerous place. It has **a** poisonous Dooklesnap plant and **an** area filled with snakes that bite. On **the** tops of **the** Twit Bushes are deadly spikes. I have **a** cat called Fluffy who likes to go in **the** garden. I am scared he will have **an** accident there! There should be **a** sign telling people how dangerous it is. Even the butterflies are **a** danger! Their wings have **an** itchy dust on them which can drop on your skin.
I look forward to hearing from you on this matter.
Mrs Grumble.

Challenge: Responses will vary, but all the words and phrases should have been used.

New Plants *Page 21*
<u>a</u> Dooklesnap Plant
<u>an</u> Ogg Bush
<u>an</u> Itwit Plant
<u>a</u> Snot Snap Plant.
Dooklesnap Plant
<u>The</u> Dooklesnap plant is <u>a</u> deadly one.
Do not touch <u>the</u> leaves or they will make you itch badly. They like to be kept in <u>a</u> very hot place but not directly in <u>the</u> sun. Plant in <u>the</u> ground when it is 4 inches high.
Gump Weed
Gump Weed grows in <u>a</u> pond.

It has <u>an</u> awful smell! It can be used in <u>a</u> nice salad or in <u>a</u> sandwich. Gump Weed takes <u>a</u> short time to grow. In <u>the</u> winter it turns purple. It is not <u>a</u> dangerous weed. When <u>the</u> weather is hot it can be used as <u>an</u> umbrella!

Dear Giantess Grunt,
Thank you for <u>the</u> beautiful Giffgo Tree. It is <u>an</u> amazing tree. I love all <u>the</u> little butterfly-shaped berries it has. I have put it in <u>a</u> cool spot in <u>the</u> garden.
I am sending you <u>a</u> cutting from my Scooter Bush Plant. It has <u>a</u> lovely smell in summer. If you squash the leaves into <u>a</u> paste, it makes <u>an</u> excellent after sun cream. It likes to be in <u>a</u> sunny spot in <u>the</u> garden. Give it <u>a</u> lot of water.
Hope to see you soon.
Love Giant Gryn xx

Challenge: Answers will vary.

Giant Gryn's Open Garden *Page 22*
The writings will vary. Children should try to be as imaginative as possible.

Mini Quiz *Page 23*
<u>A</u> sneekle rat, <u>a</u> peepo lizard, <u>an</u> eagle butterfly, a dwarf elephant, <u>a</u> bat-eared rabbit, <u>a</u> lion-headed squirrel.
I was on my way to <u>the</u> police station, when to my surprise I saw <u>a</u> huge rabbit jump out of <u>a/the</u> dustbin and run down <u>the</u> road. It was closely followed by <u>a</u> green lizard. It was <u>an</u> awful shock. The villagers were in <u>a</u> terrible flap. It seems there was <u>a</u> hole in <u>the</u> garden fence. The animals made <u>a</u> run for it. I called <u>the/an</u> animal officer who managed to catch <u>the</u> rabbit and <u>the</u> lizard and put them into <u>a</u> cage.
A <u>plain</u> scone
Plasters for my <u>heel</u>
New <u>ball</u> for the dog
<u>Piece</u> of cake
Collect <u>mail</u> from post office
Bag of <u>flour</u>
Some <u>leeks</u> for a soup
A pound of <u>meat</u>.
I drove my <u>supercar</u> on the <u>autoroute</u> to get to the <u>supermarket</u>. I bought some <u>antifreeze</u> and a great <u>autobiography</u> on 'The Life of Giantess Gom'. She is a real <u>superwoman</u>! Some people say she has <u>superpowers</u>! I bought some more <u>superglue</u> and some <u>antibiotic</u> cream for my insect bites. Then I drove home.

Captain Codfish *Page 24*
Common nouns: seas, ship, dolphins, whales, sailors, treasure, coins, jewellery, necklaces, monkey, parrot, boat, gale, mast, desert island, palm trees, jungle, natives, trees, waterfall, chest, coins, rings, jewels, bracelets
Abstract nouns: pride, joy, love, happiness.
Proper nouns: Captain Codfish, Jolly Octopus, Jim,
Mr Screecher, Beachcomber Bay.
Collective nouns: crew of sailors, tribe of natives, forest of trees.

Challenge: Stories will vary

Captain Codfish's Treasure Chest *Page 25*
Daggers, lamps, coins, brooches, chains, pearls, maps, goblets.

Challenge: **1.** anchor **2.** sail **3.** barrel
4. coconuts **5.** flag **6.** map.

Captain Codfish's Secret Map *Page 26*
Point 1: Bottlenose Bay. Point 2: Shark Reef Point 3: Cuttlefish Cove. Point 4: Lobster Lagoon. Point 5: Palm Tree Oasis. Point 6: Shipwreck Bay. Point 7: Cutlass Cavern. Point 8: Sticky Swamp.

Challenge:
Dear **R**edbeard,
It is an age since I last saw you, when we sailed on the **H**appy **S**tarfish together. **D**o you remember the battle we had in **C**uttlefish **C**ove when we sank **C**aptain **C**uttle's ship, the **S**lippery **O**ctopus? **T**hose were the days, eh! **O**ld **J**im **B**aines was in the **D**olphin **I**nn the other day. We spoke of our adventures around **S**kull **B**ay. **H**e told me that **B**ig **S**ally has a new ship called the **F**lying **A**lbatross. **S**he lives near **P**irate **C**ove.
I hope you are keeping well. **L**ook forward to seeing you soon.
Captain **C**odfish

In the Harbour *Page 27*
Boats to be circled: Anger, peace, fear, joy, love, hope.

"The Jolly Octopus was a fine ship. <u>Joy</u> filled my heart when I sailed in her. She was my <u>pride</u> and <u>love</u>. She caused <u>envy</u> amongst the other pirates I can tell you! Their eyes would flash with <u>hate</u> when I sailed into the harbour. I felt <u>sad</u> when she hit rocks in Jumbaloo during a violent storm. <u>Despair</u> filled me! <u>Anger</u> too when I thought I'd never get another ship so grand. Then, we captured the Golden Jellyfish!"

Challenge: Writing will vary.

Captain Codfish's Caverns *Page 28*
Lanterns (abstract nouns): hate, danger, joy, anger, fear, hope, love, courage.
Rocks (common nouns): octopus, fish, map, grass, boat, shell, elbow, door.

Challenge: Abstract nouns will vary. Ideas could be: rage, jealously, envy, beauty, generosity, goodness, friendship, truth, honesty, hatred.

Ye Old Sea Dog's Tavern *Page 29*
A <u>fleet</u> of ships, a <u>pride</u> of lions, a <u>litter</u> of kittens, a <u>deck</u> of cards, a <u>bunch</u> of flowers, a <u>flock</u> of birds, a <u>chest</u> of drawers, a <u>library</u> of books, a <u>flight</u> of stairs.
"It was off Cape Coddle that I saw the <u>fleet</u> of enemy ships! I had been looking at a <u>school</u> of dolphins when I saw them. We headed for the Island of Rumba where a <u>troop</u> of monkeys threw

coconuts at us. We made camp under a whole galaxy of stars. It was a wonderful sight. In the early morning a swarm of bees attacked us. Luckily we got back to the ship before we were stung. A flock of birds flew overhead as we set sail for Nunking to exchange our cargo of spices for jewels and coins."

Challenge: Diary entries will vary.

Captain Codfish's Log *Page 30*
Diary entries will vary.

Mini Quiz *Page 31*
Common nouns: parrot, island, monkey, apples, bananas, kitchen, cook, feast, shore, fire, lobsters, fish, firewood, party sea, whales.
Proper nouns: Mr Screecher, Jim, Mr Stiggle, Beachcomber Bay, Pirate Pete.
Collective Nouns: flock of parrots, bundle of firewood, pod of whales, shoal of tiny fish.
Abstract nouns: joy.

1. A <u>bunch</u> of grapes
2. A <u>litter</u> of puppies
3. A <u>library</u> of books
4. A <u>flock</u> of cows
5. A <u>deck</u> of cards

Abstract nouns: joy, anger, peace, hope.
Common nouns: ship, sand, island, shell.
Collective nouns: a pod of whales, a bunch of keys, a troop of monkeys.
Proper nouns: Mr Screecher, Coconut Cove, Pirate Pete, Captain Cork.

Bobot the Robot *Page 32*
Questions will vary. Ideas might be: How long did it take you to build Bobot? What was the hardest part of the project? How many functions does Bobot have?

Bobot the Spy *Page 33*
1. "What a marvellous party this is," said Delly Davis. "I've had a lot of fun."
2. "I've literally danced all night," squealed Lilly Lemon, "my feet are going to drop off!"
3. "I think I've talked too much," grinned Gavin Grokkle, "I can hardly speak."
4. "I thought the dancers looked amazing," gasped Gilly Jones. "Their outfits were gorgeous."
5. "I won the competition for the best outfit," smiled Lenny Luckless.
6. "I don't normally win competitions," he added.
7. "Did I leave my coat at the party?" asked Gwen Diddle.

Bobot in Japan *Page 34*
"I can cook and sew," explained Bobot. "When you are tired, I can cook supper," said Bobot. "I am programmed to be very helpful," added Bobot with a bow.
Bobot told us, "I am the most useful Robot in the world because I can do everything."
"I am able to run a bath," said Bobot, "without letting the bath water overflow!"
"Doctor Gloom is a brilliant scientist," said Bobot.

"He has programmed me so that I can do the gardening," he added. "When I am ready, I will be able to drive a car," Bobot smiled.
Ideas for the investors will vary.

Challenge: The secret conversation will vary.

Bobot the Robot Factory Tour *Page 35*
Indirect speech: Bobot explained that he had many exciting functions such as supersonic suction pads on his hands.
Bobot said that when he was tired he whirrs gently for five minutes, which gives you time to recharge him.
Bobot said that he never gets rusty which means he lasts longer.
Bobot added that Doctor Gloom is programming him to drive which will be difficult.
Bobot explained that he is easy to store. He thinks his dishwashing function is the best.

Challenge: This will vary but all the sentences should be used.

Bottville Robot Fair *Page 36*
"I think the best feature is his hoover hands," said Gary Grinling excitedly.
"How long did it take you to make Bobot?" asked Jane eagerly.
"I like the way all the dials are covered up," explained Robin Smooth.
"Will it be difficult to clean Bobot?" asked an old lady.
Daisy stared at Bobot, "he's really amazing, I love his shiny green metal; it's so pretty."

Challenge: "This is an incredible invention," said Professor Dull in amazement. "The world of housework has changed forever," he continued excitedly. Professor Edwards told the meeting, "I am so proud of Doctor Gloom, he is an amazing man." Doctor Swan said, "this robot does everything, even the washing up!" She continued, "it doesn't even get rusty in water." Professor Bird told the meeting, "Bobot is the perfect size for a robot." Professor Dull was worried, "will Bobot like being put away in a cupboard at night? He seems very human." Doctor Gloom told fellow inventors, "Bobot can also be used as a lamp so you can have him in a corner of your sitting room!"

Giving Bobot Commands *Page 37*
1. Fill the kettle with cold water from the tap.
2. Put the kettle on to boil.
3. Get the teapot out of the cupboard.
4. Put some teabags in the teapot.
5. Pour the boiling water from the kettle into the teapot.
6. Allow the tea to brew in the teapot.
7. Pour the tea into a teacup.
8. Add milk and sugar to taste.

Challenge: Instructions will vary but the imperative words in the box should be used.

Help Bobot Sort *Page 38*

Commands	Statements
Wash the dishes carefully.	We are going on holiday.
Give the dog a bath.	This fish tastes lovely.
Scrub the potatoes.	I have a new bike.
Take the tea out of the packet.	I am going to have a bath.
	The water is very hot.

Other statements and commands will vary.

Challenge: Leaflets will vary, but should have four commands and four statements.

Radio Sunshine *Page 39*

I'm called Bobot the Robot. This is my first radio interview so I'm very excited. It's the first time I've done lots of talking. Doctor Gloom is pleased with my speech. There's a special computer for my voice. I haven't done much talking until now. Doctor Gloom says he'll programme me with lots of words so that I shan't find it difficult.

isn't – is not; she'll – she will; can't – cannot; shan't – shall not; won't – will not; hasn't – has not; there's – there is; they'll – they will; isn't – is not; they're – they are.

Bobot's Malfunction *Page 40*

I was walking to the computer. I saw Doctor Gloom in his laboratory. I walked over to him. He was pleased to see me. With him was Professor Bloom. Professor Bloom looked very serious. She was wearing her special white coat. They were talking about my feet. I looked down and saw that my feet were blue. That was very upsetting.

Past tense: I was doing the washing. Bobot went to the Robot Fair. Doctor Gloom found a problem.
Present tense: I am a clever robot. Bobot is making tea. Bobot uses his long arms. Bobot is mending the plate.

Bobot's Speech *Page 41*

Present perfect statements:
I have learnt to wash up.
I have been on a train.
I have learnt how to write and read.
I have found it difficult to walk.
Doctor Gloom has spent years inventing me.
Present perfect tense:
I have been on a rollercoaster.
We have found a malfunction.
We have discovered jellyfish.
I have walked a long way today.
Doctor Gloom has been to Italy.
Bobot's nanochip has been stolen.
I have lost my ear bolts.
Other statements:
We are going on holiday.
The malfunction is serious.
My favourite colour is red.
Bobot the Robot is expensive.
Most robots cannot speak.

Challenge: Statements will vary.

Spring Cleaning *Page 42*

Statements to go in the bin:
We have found a battery booster to charge Bobot quickly.
Bobot has been targeted by evil Professor Spike.
They have given Bobot an award for being the best robot.
I have discovered the best way of keeping Bobot virus-free.
We have walked a long way.
Bobot has been my greatest invention.

Challenge: Bobot has been voted the best small domestic robot in the world. Doctor Gloom is very excited about the project. He has decided to build a more advanced version of Bobot. Projectorama will be investing £80 million to help Doctor Gloom. "We have realised that robots are very important," explained Crispin Nutter, Projectorama's Managing Director. "Bobot has been a great success," added Crispin Nutter. "Bobot is an inspiration to us all!" Projectorama have been delighted to share Doctor Gloom's new project. Doctor Gloom has not been available for comment. He has been on holiday with Bobot, taking a well-earned rest. Bobot will be going to Australia next month to show off his skills there. There has been a lot of excitement in Australia at Bobot's imminent arrival.

Stop Press! *Page 43*

News reports will vary. Past tense should be used correctly.

Mini Quiz *Page 44*

Sentences punctuated correctly are:
"I was really frightened," said Bobot tearfully.
"This was a horrible experience," sniffed Bobot.
Doctor Gloom explained, "Bobot is a very special robot."
The laboratory was covered in paper lanterns.
"It looks beautiful," exclaimed Professor Bloom happily. "I am so glad Bobot was rescued," she continued. "Bobot is a very special robot," said Professor Raven. "You should receive a prize for him," he added kindly. Doctor Gloom made a speech to his friends. "I don't like giving speeches," he told them shyly, "but I am so grateful that Bobot has returned, I want to celebrate." Tony Brown raised his glass, "to Bobot!" he said. "Welcome back!" said everyone.
Verbs: jump, sit, carry, mix, cry, stir, dance, sing.
Past tense: I went to Paris. We flew to Spain yesterday.

Police Station Problems *Page 45*

A. It is busy at the Police Station. PC Brown is having a well-earned break, because there has been so much work to do. Detective Donald has left lots of paperwork, as he is away on holiday. PC Brown has just found Mrs Woggle's dog, Tommy. Tommy is a lovely poodle, although he can be rather grumpy.

Getting to Grips with English Grammar, Year 3
© Charlotte Makhlouf and Brilliant Publications Limited

PC Brown has arrested Toni Miller, <u>who has been caught stealing watches from the jeweller.</u> Soon PC Brown will be off to the zoo, <u>where a large crocodile has gone missing</u>. PC Brown is enjoying his tea break, <u>even though all the biscuits have run out.</u> PC Brown loves biscuits, <u>especially the ones filled with chocolate and cream.</u> He has a sweet tooth, <u>which is very unhealthy for his teeth</u>.

B. Subordinate clauses will vary. Look for interesting and imaginative clauses.

Challenge: Three tourists saw Lazlo after he'd escaped, <u>although it appeared they were too frightened to speak</u>. There were claw marks by the gate, <u>which had been left open!</u> The crocodile's swamp smelt horrible, <u>due to all the rubbish.</u> I looked up frightened, <u>as a screecher monkey howled</u>. Mary, <u>a girl who had orange plaits</u>, saw Lazlo go towards the Snotsnap dogs. The Snotsnap dogs, <u>who have runny noses</u>, liked talking to Lazlo. Mrs Helga Higgins saw Lazlo at the car wash, <u>which is very alarming!</u>

Village Pet Show *Page 46*
2. Main clause: Candy's rabbit ran away
Subordinate clause: because she was scared of the balloons.
3. Main clause: The black pony ate the buns
Subordinate clause: which made Mr Henry very angry.
4. Main clause: Meggie bought a large ice-cream
Subordinate clause: who fell off her pony Twiggle.

Challenge: Sentences will vary. Children should be able to identify which is the main clause and which is the subordinate clause and use them appropriately.

PC Brown's Celebrity Mishaps *Page 47*
I was standing by the bar, <u>minding my own business</u>, when the light fell on my head.
Baybella, <u>the famous singer</u>, has lost her voice.
Frankie Donut slipped on a banana, <u>which made him sprain his ankle</u>.
<u>Even though he had a broken leg</u>, Roy Butterball insisted on dancing.

Challenge: Subordinate clauses will vary.
Suggestions might be: Gupta Popadel the famous film star: "I must go now, because I have left my supper in the oven.
Dodge Chen the famous footballer: "I have to leave now, because I have a big match tomorrow and I need a good night's sleep!"
Madge Gorm the film star: "I need to go as Poochie Woo my dog needs her medicine."

PC Brown's Day Off *Page 48*
Prepositions of place: Over, in, on, up, next to, under, between, down, above.

Challenge:
1. The fish is <u>behind</u> the seaweed.
2. The fish is <u>below</u> the seaweed.
3. The fish is <u>between</u> the seaweed.

4. The fish is <u>above</u> the seaweed.
5. The fish is <u>in front of</u> the seaweed.
6. The fish is <u>over</u> the seaweed.

Police Station Sort Out *Page 49*
His watch is <u>under</u> the books.
The biscuits are <u>on</u> the plate.
Could the files be <u>on</u> the shelf?
The telephone is <u>beside</u> the computer.
The light is <u>above</u> the picture.
The picture is <u>below</u> the light.
The cat is <u>under</u> the table.
The table is <u>above</u> the cat.
Are his keys <u>beside</u> the mug of tea?

Challenge: Stories will vary but look for the use of a wide variety of prepositions to describe where things are.

PC Brown's Reminders *Page 50*
<u>On</u> Tuesday you have a dental appointment.
PC Plod won't be back <u>until</u> 11:30am.
<u>On</u> Tuesday go to Poppleton Police Station.
I must leave work <u>by</u> 5.30pm or I will miss my bus.
A few weeks' <u>ago</u>, I went to Beech Hill School to talk to the children.
<u>Before</u> you leave for work, have a big breakfast.
<u>At</u> 3pm meet Detective Green.
At half <u>past</u> five I must feed the dog.
Remind Sally to post the letter <u>before</u> 12.00 or she will miss the post!

Challenge:
Dear PC Brown,
I am sorry to trouble you, but I was passing <u>by</u> and thought I would let you know about my missing cat, Oliver. When I got <u>in</u> from work yesterday, Oliver was not there. He often goes <u>in</u> to the cafe for some milk. But Mrs Jones <u>in</u> the cafe said he had not been <u>in/by</u>! Some time <u>ago</u>, he was not home <u>until</u> very late. If you are driving <u>past</u> my house, perhaps you could pop <u>in</u> to see me.
Yours sincerely,
Mr Evans

Goblin Caves *Page 51*
sad – miserable
eager – keen
happy – joyful
angry – cross
below – under
ugly – horrible
evil – wicked
hot – boiling
messy – untidy
smell – stink

Challenge: spiteful: unkind/nasty; untidy – chaotic; fast –quick/speedy; lovely – beautiful/gorgeous/amazing; tiny – small/minuscule/petite.
large – huge/enormous/vast/towering.

At the Dentist *Page 52*
strange – odd

junk – rubbish
tall – high
neat – tidy
ill – sick
angry – cross
wet – soaked

Words will vary for PC Brown's description of his trip to the dentist.

Suggestions are underlined: I was rather <u>terrified/alarmed/scared</u> I can tell you. Dani is very <u>sweet/kind/pleasant/agreeable</u>. I had to sit in a <u>huge/enormous/large</u> chair. Dani <u>stared/examined/scrutinised</u> (at) my teeth carefully. I don't need any fillings! She then <u>washed/scrubbed</u> my teeth for me. She had a <u>small/tiny</u> spray which tickled. When she finished she gave me a sticker for being <u>sensible/brave/nice.</u>

Challenge: Words in the teeth will vary.

Jewellery Problems *Page 53*

soft – hard
joyful – miserable
thick – thin
dainty – clumsy
boiling – freezing
rough – delicate
sour – sweet
kind – spiteful
clear – foggy
ugly – beautiful

I saw Mrs Davis, the jeweller, <u>crying/sobbing/weeping</u> in front of her shop and <u>shouting/calling/bellowing</u> for help.

There was a man in a <u>black</u> coat, <u>running/charging/scampering</u> down the road very <u>quickly/fast</u>.

When I <u>opened</u> the door, there were brooches and rings <u>messily thrown/scattered/dropped/littered</u> all over the floor.

I was so <u>upset/sad</u> when I saw the <u>huge</u> man throwing a <u>large/big</u> sack on the table that I <u>sat down</u>.

Challenge: Put the jewels in the sack. Go to the <u>broken, old</u> bridge by the <u>twisted/curved</u> pier. There's a big cafe owned by Doris. She's a <u>lovely/kind</u> old woman who has a <u>white</u> cat called Chester. Give the jewels to her under cover of <u>darkness</u>. She is expecting you at <u>dusk</u>.

To the Rescue *Page 54*
Descriptions will vary.

Mini Quiz *Page 55*
The subordinate clauses are underlined below:
1. <u>To cross the road safely,</u> always look left and right.
2. Litter attracts wild animals, <u>so pick it up and put it in a bin.</u>
3. Make sure you wear a seat belt, <u>as it could save your life.</u>
4. The kitten, <u>who was stuck up a tree,</u> was ginger.

5. The dog, <u>who was lost,</u> found its owner.
1. The squirrel is jumping <u>over</u> a rock.
2. The cat is <u>in</u> the tree.
3. The kite is flying <u>above</u> the lady.
4. The bench is <u>under</u> the dog.
5. The hat is <u>on</u> the lady's head.
6. The kite is <u>up</u> in the sky.

Slippery Sam is very <u>mean/nasty</u>. This has been a very <u>eventful</u> day. I would like a <u>boiling/warm</u> cup of tea. I wonder if we might <u>trap/capture/snare</u> the jewellery thief!
1. I am going to the zoo <u>after</u> I have been to the park.
2. <u>On</u> Friday I am going to the theatre.
3. I will be back at the station <u>before</u> it closes.
4. The cafe closes at <u>around</u> 6pm.

The Grand Opening *Page 56*
Challenge: <u>After</u> a nice breakfast, why not head off to the lake. <u>When</u> you get there, take a canoe and go exploring. <u>As soon as/After/Once</u> you finish, you can go swimming or fishing. The lake is beautiful <u>as</u> you will find out! Stroll through the forest <u>until</u> it is time for lunch. <u>While</u> you are having lunch in the Squirrel Cafe, look out for wildlife. You can hire a bike for a <u>while</u>. Why not ride around <u>until</u> it gets dark?

Treetop Walkway *Page 57*
I thought it was brilliant <u>even though</u> I was a bit scared.
The view was beautiful <u>because</u> we were so high up.
I wanted to go round twice <u>but</u> Mum said no!
The Tree Top Walkway is open all day but not at night.
We took the wrong turning as a result we didn't get to the Tree Top Cafe.
We saw squirrels and deer even though they ran away from us.
We walked to the end until we got to the lake and then we stopped.

Challenge: Comments for Granny and Grandad Green will vary.

Holiday Park Rules *Page 58*
Please keep to the paths, <u>otherwise</u> you might slip.
Our trees are ancient <u>so</u> please don't climb them.
Shoes should always be worn on the walkways <u>so</u> you do not hurt your feet.
<u>Because</u> this is a conservation area, please do not chase or frighten the wildlife.
<u>When/After</u> hiring your bike, get a map of the area so you don't get lost.
Barbecues are not allowed <u>since/because</u> they may start a forest fire.
Quad Biking: Fasten your helmet <u>as soon as/once/when</u> you get on the bike.
Spa and Sauna: <u>While</u> you are relaxing, why not have a cool drink.
Challenge: We want you to have a happy stay

because we value your custom. <u>Whenever</u> you need help, please ask our staff for assistance. <u>Since</u> our grand opening, we have made a new spa. We have activities for adults <u>and</u> children.

Forest Park Activities *Page 59*
Adverbs will vary but here are some suggestions:
"I loved the water slide!" giggled Benny <u>happily/excitedly.</u>
"I had a beautiful walk," said Grandpa Green <u>contentedly/happily/delightedly.</u>
"The fishing was amazing!" squeaked Tilly <u>enthusiastically/excitedly.</u>
"Four hours at the spa," sighed Mrs Lewis <u>contentedly/peacefully/wistfully.</u>
"We saw deer!" shouted Eric <u>loudly.</u>
"I must admit I was frightened on the Treetop Walkway," whispered Granny Green <u>nervously/fearfully.</u>
"That bike ride was exhausting," muttered Harry <u>miserably/wearily.</u>

Challenge: Adverbs: slowly, carefully, excitedly, nearly, excitedly, quickly, enormously, energetically, happily, miserably, unhappily.

At the Reception Desk *Page 60*
Adverbs will vary, some ideas might be:
"I was really hoping for three tickets," moaned Alfie <u>miserably/despairingly/crossly.</u>
"There's a new water slide!" shouted Dilly <u>excitedly/happily/loudly.</u>
Sally sobbed <u>sadly/inconsolably,</u> "but I wanted to see the beach!"
"Four tickets for the Salsa Show!" announced Derek <u>pompously/proudly/loftily/loudly.</u>
"I can't believe there are no bikes left!" exclaimed Mrs Flagg <u>crossly/angrily/bossily.</u>
"Oh no!" squeaked May <u>excitedly/nervously,</u> "I've dropped my sunglasses!"
Ideas for what Tina might be saying will vary.
Suggestions might be:
<u>"What do you mean the linen has been dyed purple!"</u> snapped Tina crossly.
<u>"We will move you to another room immediately,"</u> began Tina quickly.
<u>"There's been a fire in the forest,"</u> began Tina quickly.
<u>"It's on the third floor,"</u> said Tina patiently.
<u>"Which show did you want to see,"</u> said Tina patiently.
<u>"If I could ask you all to leave the Squirrel Restaurant by the emergency exit,"</u> announced Tina calmly.

Challenge: Tina's thoughts will vary.

Theatre Production *Page 61*
This is <u>absolutely</u> disgraceful!
This is a <u>really/very/extremely</u> difficult situation!
Everyone is <u>terribly/extremely</u> worried about their things.
Gareth, the show's Director, is <u>absolutely</u> furious

about the missing props.
"This is all <u>terribly/extremely/very</u> distressing," moaned Gareth.
1. absolutely, terribly
2. extremely, very
3. really
4. understandably.

Challenge: "Look everyone," began Gareth calmly. "I know you're really upset, but we will find the props." Melba Coast began grumbling <u>unhappily</u>. "This is <u>terribly</u> annoying," she snapped <u>crossly</u>. "I don't need my hat," said Tamsin <u>quickly</u>. "I can do without it." In the dressing room, Mrs Evans was crying <u>noisily</u>. "This is <u>extremely</u> bad," she sniffed <u>miserably</u>. "They all blame me! Of course I'm <u>understandably</u> upset." Crispin Crust has been searching <u>furiously</u> for his parchment letter. He is <u>extremely</u> cross. "I'm <u>really</u> desperate for that letter," he shouted <u>nastily</u>. Gareth is speaking <u>quickly</u> to Dorian Whisp, the stage manager, who is <u>terribly</u> worried. "We can't do the sword fight without the swords," he explained <u>miserably</u>.

Dillcombe Bay *Page 62*
Dillcombe Bay Smugglers
<u>When/Before</u> I was born, there used to be smugglers along this coast. <u>Whenever/When</u> there was no moon they would head for shore. <u>As soon as</u> it was dark, they would land their goods. <u>Once</u> ashore, the cargo was hidden away in caves and caverns. <u>Whenever</u> I walk along the beach I remember the old smugglers! But <u>since</u> then no smugglers have been spotted in this area.
Fossil Hunts
<u>Whenever</u> we can, we hold fossil hunts along the beach. <u>Once</u> there used to be dinosaurs here! <u>Since</u> then, we have always looked for fossils. <u>As soon as</u> the tide goes out, you can start hunting! <u>Whenever</u> I find a fossil, I get very excited. <u>While</u> I hunt for fossils, my wife fishes in the sea. <u>After</u> a long day fossil hunting, we return home!
Postcards will vary.

At the Water Park *Page 63*
<u>Before</u> using the mega slide, please listen to the safety instructions.
<u>As soon as</u> you have been down the slide, please move out of the way quickly.
<u>Once</u> the slide is clear, you may go down.
<u>Before</u> swimming, please take a shower.
<u>Whenever</u> the whistle blows, please listen to the lifeguard.

Challenge: Posters will vary. Adverbs of time should be used.

At the Beach *Page 64*
1. Consequently: because she didn't listen she fell.
2. Therefore: wear suncream or you will burn.
3. However: watch out for the seagulls or they will eat your food.
4. Because: wear a life jacket or you might drown.

Challenge: The problems will vary, however, look for the correct use of adverbs.

New Fossil Discovered *Page 65*
Articles for the newspaper will all be different. The children should be imaginative and they should use the ideas to help them.

Challenge: This will also be different.

Mini Quiz *Page 66*
The Forest Cabin
Choose to stay in a forest cabin <u>because</u> it is fun to be in the forest. <u>Even though</u> they are set in the woods, they are not far from the main building. Forest cabins are great for families <u>because</u> they are nice and big.

The Tree Top House
<u>Even though</u> they are high up, the steps are easy to climb. Great for couples <u>because</u> they are small. Watch the wildlife on the lake <u>until</u> the sun goes down. They are not suitable for small children <u>but</u> they are good for teenagers!

Woodland Pod Dwelling
Our visitors wanted to be close to the wildlife. <u>Consequently</u>, we designed the Woodland Pod! <u>Even though</u> it looks small, it has lots of room inside. There is a kitchen, a bathroom <u>but</u> no television! Sentences with adverbs will vary.

Trouble in Giantville *Page 67*
Challenge: Children should think of a good headline and design an appropriate picture.

Newspaper Features *Page 68*
Headlines, pictures, captions for the pictures will all vary. The ideas should relate to the writing.
Ideas for headline: Home sweet Home; Gogg finishes Dream Home.
Ideas for headline: Village Destroyed: Dipple Destroyed; Dipple Accidentally Squashed.

Challenge: The articles will all be different. Challenge the children to give as many details as possible; they can extend their abilities by adding witness comments.

Fashion Feature *Page 69*
I am thrilled to show you my beautiful new range of clothing for giants. I have been designing the range of clothing for the last two years in my mountain top studio.

I have used spiders as my inspiration because they spin such lovely, delicate, yet strong webs. I want my clothes to look delicate and beautiful too as well as be strong enough for tough giant use.

My latest collection features some pretty swim wear, some beautiful day wear, as well as some ballgowns and suits for men. My next collection will be focusing on clothing for work.

Challenge: The additional paragraphs will vary but they should relate to the article.

Giant's Weekly Letters *Page 70*
Dear Giantess Gringle,

Thank you for your letter about the recent troll situation. Many of my friends are trolls and they are very sad about the latest troll troubles.

We are hoping to hold a small fireworks party next week to celebrate the harvest festival, to which all trolls and giants are invited. We hold a fireworks party every year so we hope that you can come.

On another note, were you aware that there are a lot of trolls who are trying to gather together to discuss the troubles. They want to meet at the Grym Hotel next week. We hope you can be there too.
With Best Wishes
Giant Groan

Dear Grimbal,

We were very interested to hear about your recent adventures in the green Horn Mountains. It is exciting to hear that there are Cookweed birds living there.

I have written to the head of the Cookweed Society who is planning to send an expert to the Mountains. He would be pleased to meet you there.

This is an exciting find and we would love you to write an article for the Giant's Weekly paper all about the Cookweed birds you have discovered.
I look forward to hearing from you.
With Best Wishes
Giant Groan

Challenge: Letters will vary. Encourage more able children to write four or five paragraphs and extend their writing through the use of subordinate clauses.

Under the Mountain *Page 71*
Trolls are known for being fierce and warlike. However, there are some trolls who live a peaceful life under the mountains. These trolls enjoy making beautiful jewellery and carving pictures into their walls.

Most trolls have quick tempers and jump into fights without thinking. Their swords are sharp and deadly and they learn to fight from a young age.

Troll children go to school from the age of five where they learn to read and write and compose songs.

Challenge: Additional paragraphs should relate to food and free time. Encourage subordinate clauses to expand the sentences and improve the content.

All About Giantville *Page 72–73*
Headings
Possible ideas could be: Giantville, Giantania's Oldest Town; Giantville's Best Baker; The Best Bread for 20 Years.

Challenge: Ideas and information on teeth will vary. Possible ideas: Heading: Celebrity Giants; Local Giants; About Giantville.

1st subheading: Books in Giantville; Local Writer Giant Gwin.
2nd subheading: Gardening in Giantville; Garden Art; Beautiful Gardens.

Challenge: Writing will vary. Encourage imaginative ideas.

The Giant's Express Newspaper *Page 74*
Exclamations: Watch out!
2 Million year old giant skeleton found!
Riots in Giantville reach third day!
Local giant in avalanche horror!
Commands: Put the rubbish in the bin.
Take the watering can to the shed.
Statements: This is a good day for giants.
There will be a day of celebration.
The young giant said it was a foolish thing to do.
It is believed that the two giants were not guilty.
Questions: Why did you do it?
Did you take the flowers?

Challenge: Choice of statements will vary and the writing around it will also vary.

The Miracle of Giantville *Page 75*
The Miracle of Giantville
Do you believe in miracles? <u>One</u> dark night a young giantess called Gwinda was lost in the <u>forest</u>. <u>She</u> had no idea <u>where</u> she was. <u>All</u> of a sudden she <u>thought</u> she felt gentle hands pushing her away. <u>She</u> was so tired, she fell asleep against a tree. <u>In</u> the morning she realised she was literally a few feet away from a terrible <u>cliff</u>! <u>"I could</u> have fallen down <u>it,"</u> she said, <u>"if</u> it hadn't been for those strange hands pushing me. It was a miracle<u>! I</u> built my home not far from the cliff and called it <u>Grimlock</u>. Other giants came and settled here <u>too</u> and so <u>Giantville</u> was born. "
Win a Holiday!
<u>Win</u> a holiday to the Giantania Coast. <u>Swim</u> with <u>dolphins</u> and go fishing on the <u>sea</u>. This is a <u>great</u> opportunity to relax and recharge <u>your batteries</u>.
Text: GIANTWIN23 to GIANT HOLIDAYS.
Giant Ice-cream
Fabulous Flavours is a new ice <u>-cream</u> <u>shop</u> for giants in <u>Giantville</u>. <u>Choose</u> from a variety of new and exciting <u>flavours</u>. Why not try <u>gooseberry delight</u> or lavender and ginger <u>cream</u>. Try our fabulous flavours<u>!</u>

Challenge: Advertisements will vary. Ensure that the children proofread their work carefully.

Trolls Wanted *Page 76*
A <u>small, red-faced</u> troll with <u>bright orange</u> hair was spotted raiding a garden shed. The troll is believed to have <u>big</u> hands and <u>pointed</u> ears. He was wearing a <u>brown</u> jacket, <u>red-checked</u> shirt, <u>blue</u> trousers and <u>big, heavy black</u> boots. Last seen carrying a <u>cream-coloured, canvas</u> sack believed to be filled with garden tools.
A <u>short, black-haired</u> troll, wearing a <u>green</u> and <u>red spotted</u> dress and <u>blue</u> boots. The troll was seen

carrying <u>two beautiful, yellow</u> Sneakle Roses in her arms whilst on her back she had a <u>black</u> rucksack filled with <u>small</u> garden tools.
REWARD: 25 gold pieces.

Challenge: The wanted poster will vary, but plenty of interesting adjectives should be encouraged.

At the Garden Centre *Page 77*
This <u>beautiful, majestic</u> Loopal Plant will be a <u>wonderful</u> addition to your garden. It loves <u>cool, shady</u> places and a little bit of <u>bright</u> sunlight. Take home a <u>gorgeous, fluffy</u> Weeping Whistle Bush. Its <u>sweet</u> singing will echo around your garden. In Summer, they bear <u>tiny, orange</u> berries which can be crushed to make a <u>delicious, tangy</u> jam.
Descriptions of the three plants should vary. Encourage the use of adjectives to describe the plant. Perhaps the children could draw pictures of them to help their descriptions.

Challenge: Posters will vary.

Troll Troubles Worsen *Page 78*
Six paragraphs were used.
Similes are underlined below:
The troll crisis increased last night as a group of trolls went <u>as mad as monkeys</u> in Giantville, setting fire to sheds and looting shops.
Local giants were alarmed as eight trolls ran rampage around the town <u>screaming like banshees</u>, breaking shop windows, looting and setting fire to garden sheds. "I watched them saunter into town <u>as cool as cucumbers</u>," Giant Goff told reporters. "They charged into my garden <u>as bold as brass</u> and set fire to my shed! I was <u>as mad as a hatter</u>!"
Mayor Grumble helped the Giant Police to get the trolls out of town. "They were screaming and yelling, their eyes <u>as black as coal</u>," explained Mayor Grumble. "They smirked at us looking <u>as pleased as punch</u> as they broke two shop windows. PC Giant Greebly stood <u>as strong as an oak</u> and roared at them to leave."
Trolls are known to be difficult creatures. One minute they look <u>as sweet as pie</u>, the next minute they look <u>as mean as snakes</u>.
After a night of worry and <u>watching the trolls like hawks</u>, the Giantville Police were finally able to get rid of them. A 24 hour watch has been put in place and road blocks have been set up to protect Giantville.
Normally <u>as gentle as lambs</u>, the giants are now angry and want justice.

Challenge: Children should be encouraged to use all the similes and be inventive and creative when using them.

Troll Talk *Page 79*
Similes: 1. as mad as hatters; 2. as cool as cucumbers; 3. like cats and dogs; 4. as hard as nails; 5. like a dog with a bone; 6. as cold as ice.
Ideas for similes – encourage the children to have

fun and be creative:
as pretty <u>as a doll/as a cake</u>
as cheeky <u>as a monkey/chicken/rat</u>
as sweet <u>as candy/sugar</u>
as clever <u>as a fox/hawk</u>
as soft <u>as fur/silk/a rabbit's tail</u>
as fiery <u>as a volcano/red hot chilli peppers/tabasco sauce</u>
as smooth <u>as paper/a strawberry smoothie</u>.

Challenge: Similes and the way in which they are used will vary.

Giants at Home Magazine *Page 80*
Metaphors: Faster than lightning; the snow was a white blanket; a breath of fresh air; the wind was an angry witch; the stars were sparkling diamonds.
Challenge: Metaphors will vary.

The Troll Times *Page 81*
Newspaper headings, pictures and captions will vary. Encourage the use of reported speech for the article.

Challenge: Advertisements will also vary but they should be relevant to the article.

Mini Quiz *Page 82*
This is amazing! (exclamation mark)
Are you coming to Giantville? (question mark)
This has been a difficult time for the giants. (statement)
Did you buy me a Giant's Weekly? (question mark)
Stop that! (command)
Get out of Giantville! (exclamation mark)
Metaphors: The sun was a burning light. Her eyes were shining stars. The wind was an angry witch.
Similes: As quick as lightning, he pounced. His eyes were as hard as nails. Her heart was as cold as ice.

9 781783 172177